THE 10 BEST

BAR FIGHTING MOVES

SAMMY FRANCO

Also by Sammy Franco

Cane Fighting
Double End Bag Training
The Heavy Bag Bible
The Widow Maker Compendium
Invincible: Mental Toughness Techniques for Peak Performance
Unleash Hell: A Step-by-Step Guide to Devastating Widow Maker Combinations
Feral Fighting: Advanced Widow Maker Fighting Techniques
The Widow Maker Program: Extreme Self-Defense for Deadly Force Situations
Savage Street Fighting: Tactical Savagery as a Last Resort
Heavy Bag Workout
Heavy Bag Combinations
Heavy Bag Training
The Complete Body Opponent Bag Book
Stand and Deliver: A Street Warrior's Guide to Tactical Combat Stances
Maximum Damage: Hidden Secrets Behind Brutal Fighting Combinations
First Strike: End a Fight in Ten Seconds or Less!
The Bigger They Are, The Harder They Fall
Self-Defense Tips and Tricks
Kubotan Power: Quick & Simple Steps to Mastering the Kubotan Keychain
Gun Safety: For Home Defense and Concealed Carry
Out of the Cage: A Guide to Beating a Mixed Martial Artist on the Street
Warrior Wisdom: Inspiring Ideas from the World's Greatest Warriors
War Machine: How to Transform Yourself Into a Vicious and Deadly Street Fighter
1001 Street Fighting Secrets
When Seconds Count: Self-Defense for the Real World
Killer Instinct: Unarmed Combat for Street Survival
Street Lethal: Unarmed Urban Combat

The 10 Best Bar Fighting Moves (The 10 Best Book Series #9)
Copyright © 2017 by Sammy Franco
ISBN: 978-1-941845-43-1
Printed in the United States of America

Published by Contemporary Fighting Arts, LLC.
Visit us Online at: **SammyFranco.com**

For author interviews or publicity information, please send inquiries in care of the publisher.

Contents

"Approach combat in terms of black and white, but always be prepared for gray."

– Sammy Franco

Warning!

The self-defense techniques, tactics, methods, and information described and depicted in this book can be dangerous and could result in serious injury and or death and should not be used or practiced in any way without the guidance of a professional reality based self-defense instructor.

The author, publisher, and distributors of this book disclaim any liability from loss, injury, or damage, personal or otherwise, resulting from the information and procedures in this book. *This book is for academic study only.*

Before you begin any exercise program, including those suggested in this book, it is important to check with your physician to see if you have any condition that might be aggravated by strenuous exercise.

Why You Should Read This Book!

To most people, *bar fighting* immediately conjures up images of inebriated bums throwing blows at each other. To others, it's a bunch of belligerent and testosterone-fueled men acting like children, often with the goal of impressing a woman. Regardless of how you see it, bar fighting is a potentially deadly threat to the average law-abiding citizen.

As a self-defense expert, I'm well acquainted with bars and nightclubs. In fact, I've worked in the bar business for well over a decade, and most of that time I was employed as a bouncer or doorman.

During those ten years, I've worked in all types of watering holes - from the ritzy exclusive nightclubs to seedy strip clubs; I've seen it all and can tell you that bar fighting has deadly consequences.

Here's a true story that took place several weeks after I stopped working as a head bouncer at a Gentleman's Club in Washington, DC. A few weeks after I quit, a new head doorman was hired and was later viciously murdered by one of the patrons. However, what's even more disturbing was the manner in which the bouncer was attacked.

Apparently, after being thrown out of the club for taking photos of a nude dancer, an enraged patron later returned with a can of gasoline and attempted to set the place on fire. When the twenty-six-year-old bouncer tried to stop him, the enraged patron doused him with gasoline and set him on fire.

As a result, the bouncer suffered critical burns to 90% of his body, requiring him to undergo dozens of painful surgical procedures. Subsequently, the bouncer died from his injuries, and the patron was sentenced to thirty-five years in prison for arson and murder.

Unfortunately, this is just one of the many disturbing cautionary tales of violence that takes place every day in drinking establishments.

The 10 Best Bar Fighting Moves: Down and Dirty Fighting Techniques to Save Your Ass When Things Get Ugly is a concise guide designed to teach some of the most effective bar fighting techniques for self-defense.

These unique bar fighting skills can be performed by just about anyone, young and old, regardless of size or strength or level of experience. Most importantly, you don't need martial arts training to master these practical and effective fighting techniques.

Unlike other self-defense books, this text is devoid of tricky or flashy fighting moves that can get you injured or possibly killed when defending against a seasoned or determined attacker. Instead, it arms you with practical and deceptive fighting techniques that work in the chaos of real-life assaults. In fact, the skills and maneuvers found in these pages are surprisingly simple and easy to apply.

Beware, the information and techniques contained herein are dangerous and should only be used to protect yourself or a loved one from the immediate risk of unlawful injury. Remember, the decision to use physical force must always be a last resort, after all other means of avoiding violence have been exhausted.

Finally, The 10 Best Bar Fighting Moves is based on some of the concepts featured in my other best selling book. Therefore, if you desire a more in-depth study of this subject, I suggest taking a look into some of these works.

Train hard and be safe!

Sammy Franco

Introduction
Contemporary Fighting Arts

The 10 Best Bar Fighting Moves

Exploring Contemporary Fighting Arts

Before diving head first into this book, I'd like to first introduce you to my unique system of fighting, Contemporary Fighting Arts. I hope it will give you a greater understanding and appreciation of the material in this book.

Contemporary Fighting Arts® (CFA), is a state-of-the-art combat system that was introduced to the world in 1983. This sophisticated and practical system of self-defense is designed specifically to provide efficient and effective methods to avoid, defuse, confront, and neutralize both armed and unarmed assailants in a variety of deadly situations and circumstances.

Unlike karate, kung-fu, mixed martial arts and the like, CFA is the first offensive-based American martial art that is specifically designed for the violence that plagues our cruel city streets. CFA dispenses with the extraneous and the impractical and focuses on real-life street fighting.

Every tool, technique and tactic found within the CFA system must meet three essential criteria for fighting: efficiency, effectiveness, and safety. Efficiency means that the techniques permit you to reach your combative objective quickly and economically. Effectiveness means that the elements of the system will produce the desired effect. Finally, Safety means that the combative elements provide the least amount of danger and risk for you - the fighter.

CFA is not about mind-numbing tournaments or senseless competition. It does not require you to waste time and energy practicing forms (katas) or other impractical rituals. There are no theatrical kicks or exotic techniques. Finally, CFA does not adhere blindly to tradition for tradition's sake. Simply put, it is a scientific yet pragmatic approach to staying alive on the streets.

CFA has been taught to people of all walks of life. Some include the U.S. Border Patrol, police officers, deputy sheriffs, security guards, military personnel, private investigators, surgeons, lawyers, college professors, airline pilots, as well as black belts, boxers, and kick boxers. CFA's broad appeal results from its ability to teach people how to really fight.

It's All In The Name!

Before discussing the three components that make up Contemporary Fighting Arts, it is important to understand how CFA acquired its unique name. To begin, the first word, "Contemporary," was selected because it refers to the system's modern, up-to-date orientation. Unlike traditional martial arts, CFA is specifically designed to meet the challenges of our modern world.

The second term, "Fighting," was chosen because it accurately describes the system's combat orientation. After all, why not just call it Contemporary Martial Arts? There are two reasons for this. First, the word "martial" conjures up images of traditional and impractical martial art forms that are antithetical to the system. Second, why dilute a perfectly functional name when the word "fighting" defines the system so succinctly? Contemporary Fighting Arts is about teaching people how to really fight.

Let's look at the last word, "Arts." In the subjective sense, "art" refers to the combat skills that are acquired through arduous study, practice, and observation. The bottom line is that effective street fighting skills will require consistent practice and attention. Take, for example, something as seemingly basic as an elbow strike, which will actually require hundreds of hours of practice to perfect.

The pluralization of the word "Art" reflects CFA's protean

instruction. The various components of CFA's training (i.e., firearms training, stick fighting, ground fighting, natural body weapon mastery, and so on) have all truly earned their status as individual art forms and, as such, require years of consistent study and practice to perfect. To acquire a greater understanding of CFA, here is an overview of the system's three vital components: the physical, the mental, and the spiritual.

Police officers need practical and effective defensive tactics for dealing with violent street criminals. This is why many law enforcement officers seek out Contemporary Fighting Arts training.

The Physical Component

The physical component of CFA focuses on the physical development of a fighter, including physical fitness, weapon and technique mastery, and self-defense attributes.

Physical Fitness

If you are going to prevail in a street fight, you must be physically fit. It's that simple. In fact, you will never master the tools and skills of combat unless you're in excellent physical shape. On the average, you will have to spend more than an hour a day to achieve maximum fitness.

In CFA physical fitness comprises the following three broad components: cardiorespiratory conditioning, muscular/skeletal conditioning, and proper body composition.

The cardiorespiratory system includes the heart, lungs, and circulatory system, which undergo tremendous stress during the course of a street fight. So you're going to have to run, jog, bike, swim, or skip rope to develop sound cardiorespiratory conditioning. Each aerobic workout should last a minimum of 30 minutes and be performed at least four times per week.

The second component of physical fitness is muscular/skeletal conditioning. In the streets, the strong survive and the rest go to the morgue. To strengthen your bones and muscles to withstand the rigors of a real fight, your program must include progressive resistance (weight training) and calisthenics. You will also need a stretching program designed to loosen up every muscle group. You can't kick, punch, ground fight, or otherwise execute the necessary body mechanics if you're "tight" or inflexible. Stretching on a regular basis will also increase the muscles' range of motion, improve circulation, reduce the possibility of injury, and relieve daily stress.

The final component of physical fitness is proper body composition: simply, the ratio of fat to lean body tissue. Your diet and training regimen will affect your level or percentage of body fat significantly. A sensible and consistent exercise program accompanied by a healthy and balanced diet will facilitate proper body composition. Do not neglect this important aspect of physical fitness.

Weapon and Technique Mastery

You won't stand a chance against a vicious assailant if you don't master the weapons and tools of fighting. In CFA, we teach our students both armed and unarmed methods of combat. Unarmed fighting requires that you master a complete arsenal of natural body weapons and techniques. In conjunction, you must also learn the various stances, hand positioning, footwork, body mechanics, defensive structure, locks, chokes, and various holds. Keep in mind that something as simple as a basic punch will actually require hundreds of hours to perfect.

Range proficiency is another important aspect of weapon and technique mastery. Briefly, range proficiency is the ability to fight effectively in all three ranges of unarmed fighting. Although punching range tools are emphasized in CFA, kicking and grappling ranges cannot be neglected. Our kicking range tools consist of deceptive and powerful low-line kicks. Grappling range tools include head-butts, elbows, knees, foot stomps, biting, tearing, gouging, and crushing tactics.

Although CFA focuses on striking, we also teach our students a myriad of chokes, locks, and holds that can be used in a ground fight. While such grappling range submission techniques are not the most preferred methods of dealing with a ground fighting situation, they must be studied for the following six reasons: (1) level of force - many ground fighting situations do not justify the use of deadly force. In such instances, you must apply various non-lethal submission holds, (2) nature of the beast - in order to escape any choke, lock or hold, you must first know how to apply them yourself, (3) occupational requirement- some professional occupations (police, security, etc.) require that you possess a working knowledge of various submission techniques, (4) subduing a friend or relative - in many cases it is best to restrain and control a friend or relative with a submission hold instead of striking him with a natural body weapon, (5) anatomical orientation - practicing various chokes, locks and holds will help you develop a strong orientation of the human anatomy, and (6) refutation requirement - finally, if you are going to criticize the combative limitations of any submission hold, you better be sure that you can perform it yourself.

Contemporary Fighting Arts is more than a self defense system, its a one-of-a-kind martial arts style geared for real world self defense.

Defensive tools and skills are also taught. Our defensive structure is efficient, uncomplicated, and impenetrable. It provides the fighter maximum protection while allowing complete freedom of choice for acquiring offensive control. Our defensive structure is based on distance, parrying, blocking, evading, mobility, and stance structure.

Simplicity is always the key.

Students are also instructed in specific methods of armed fighting. For example, CFA provides instruction about firearms for personal and household protection. We provide specific guidelines for handgun purchasing, operation, nomenclature, proper caliber, shooting fundamentals, cleaning, and safe storage. Our firearm program also focuses on owner responsibility and the legal ramifications regarding the use of deadly force.

CFA's weapons program also consists of natural body weapons, knives and edged weapons, single and double stick, makeshift weaponry, the side-handle baton, and oleoresin capsicum (OC) spray.

Combat Attributes

Your offensive and defensive tools are useless unless they are used strategically. For any tool or technique to be effective in a real fight, it must be accompanied by specific attributes. Attributes are qualities that enhance a particular tool, technique, or maneuver. Some examples include speed, power, timing, coordination, accuracy, non-telegraphic movement, balance, and target orientation.

CFA also has a wide variety of training drills and methodologies designed to develop and sharpen these combat attributes. For example, our students learn to ground fight while blindfolded, spar with one arm tied down, and fight while handcuffed.

Reality is the key. For example, in class students participate in full-contact exercises against fully padded assailants, and real weapon disarms are rehearsed and analyzed in a variety of dangerous scenarios. Students also train with a large variety of equipment, including heavy bags, double-end bags, uppercut bags, pummel bags, focus mitts, striking shields, mirrors, rattan sticks, foam and plastic bats, kicking pads, knife drones, trigger-sensitive (mock) guns, boxing and digit gloves, full-body armor, and hundreds of different environmental props.

There are more than two hundred unique training methodologies used in Contemporary Fighting Arts. Each one is scientifically designed to prepare students for the hard-core realities of real world combat. There are also three specific training methodologies used to develop and sharpen the fundamental attributes and skills of armed and unarmed fighting, including proficiency training, conditioning training, and street training.

CFA has a several unique military combat training programs. Our mission is to provide today's modern soldier with the knowledge, skills and attitude necessary to survive a wide variety of real world combat scenarios. Our military program is designed to provide the modern soldier with the safest and most effective skills and tactics to control and decentralize armed and unarmed enemies.

Proficiency training can be used for both armed and unarmed skills. When conducted properly, proficiency training develops speed, power, accuracy, non-telegraphic movement, balance, and general psychomotor skill. The training objective is to sharpen one specific body weapon, maneuver, or technique at a time by executing it over and over for a prescribed number of repetitions. Each time the technique or maneuver is executed with "clean" form at various speeds. Movements are also performed with the eyes closed to develop a kinesthetic "feel" for the action. Proficiency training can be accomplished through the use of various types of equipment, including the heavy bag, double-end bag, focus mitts, training knives, real and mock pistols, striking shields, shin and knee guards, foam and plastic bats, mannequin heads, and so on.

Conditioning training develops endurance, fluidity, rhythm, distancing, timing, speed, footwork, and balance. In most cases, this type of training requires the student to deliver a variety of fighting combinations for three- or four-minute rounds separated by 30-second breaks. Like proficiency training, this type of training can also be performed at various speeds. A good workout consists of at least five rounds. Conditioning training can be performed on the bags with full-contact sparring gear, rubber training knives, focus mitts, kicking shields, and shin guards, or against imaginary assailants in shadow fighting.

Conditioning training is not necessarily limited to just three- or four-minute rounds. For example, CFA's ground fighting training can last as long as 30 minutes. The bottom line is that it all depends on what you are training for.

Street training is the final preparation for the real thing. Since many violent altercations are explosive, lasting an average of 20 seconds, you must prepare for this possible scenario. This means delivering explosive and powerful compound attacks with vicious intent for approximately 20 seconds, resting one minute, and then repeating the process.

Street training prepares you for the stress and immediate fatigue of a real fight. It also develops speed, power, explosiveness, target selection and recognition, timing, footwork, pacing, and breath control. You should practice this methodology in different lighting, on different terrains, and in different environmental settings. You can use different types of training equipment as well. For example, you can prepare yourself for multiple assailants by having your training partners attack you with focus mitts from a variety of angles, ranges, and target postures. For 20 seconds, go after them with vicious low-line kicks, powerful punches, and devastating strikes.

When all is said and done, the physical component creates a fighter who is physically fit and armed with a lethal arsenal of tools, techniques, and weapons that can be deployed with destructive results.

The Mental Component

The mental component of CFA focuses on the cerebral aspects of a fighter, developing killer instinct, strategic/tactical awareness, analysis and integration skills, philosophy, and cognitive skills.

The Killer Instinct

Deep within each of us is a cold and deadly primal power known as the "killer instinct." The killer instinct is a vicious combat mentality that surges to your consciousness and turns you into a fierce fighter who is free of fear, anger, and apprehension. If you want to survive the horrifying dynamics of real criminal violence, you must cultivate and utilize this instinctive killer mentality.

There are 14 characteristics of CFA's killer instinct. They are: (1) clear and lucid thinking, (2) heightened situational awareness, (3) adrenaline surge, (4) mobilized body, (5) psychomotor control, (6) absence of distraction, (7) tunnel vision, (8) fearless mind-set, (9) tactical implementation, (10) the lack of emotion, (11) breath control, (12) pseudospeciation, (13) viciousness, and (14) pain tolerance.

Visualization and crisis rehearsal are just two techniques used to develop, refine, and channel this extraordinary source of strength and energy so that it can be used to its full potential.

Strategic/Tactical Awareness

Strategy is the bedrock of preparedness. In CFA, there are three unique categories of strategic awareness that will diminish the likelihood of criminal victimization. They are criminal awareness, situational awareness, and self-awareness. When developed, these essential skills prepare you to assess a wide variety of threats instantaneously and accurately. Once you've made a proper threat assessment, you will be able to choose one of the following five self-defense options: comply, escape, de-escalate, assert, or fight back.

CFA also teaches students to assess a variety of other important factors, including the assailant's demeanor, intent, range, positioning and weapon capability, as well as such environmental issues as escape routes, barriers, terrain, and makeshift weaponry. In addition to assessment skills, CFA also teaches students how to enhance perception and observation skills.

Analysis and Integration Skills

The analytical process is intricately linked to understanding how to defend yourself in any threatening situation. If you want to be the best, every aspect of fighting and personal protection must be dissected. Every strategy, tactic, movement, and concept must be broken down to its atomic parts. The three planes (physical, mental, spiritual) of self-defense must be unified scientifically through arduous practice and constant exploration.

CFA's most advanced practitioners have sound insight and understanding of a wide range of sciences and disciplines. They include human anatomy, kinesiology, criminal justice, sociology, kinesics, proxemics, combat physics, emergency medicine, crisis management, histrionics, police and military science, the psychology of aggression, and the role of archetypes.

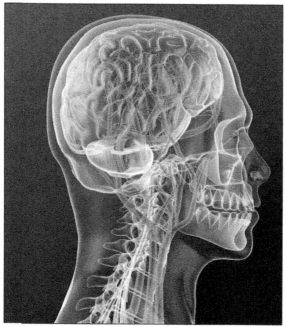

CFA's mental component focuses on the cognitive development of a fighter, including strategic/tactical awareness, analysis and integration, cognitive skills, the killer instinct, and philosophy.

Analytical exercises are also a regular part of CFA training. For example, we conduct problem-solving sessions involving particular assailants attacking in defined environments. We move hypothetical attackers through various ranges to provide insight into tactical solutions. We scrutinize different methods of attack for their general utility in combat. We also discuss the legal ramifications of self-defense on a frequent basis.

In addition to problem-solving sessions, students are slowly exposed to concepts of integration and modification. Oral and written examinations are given to measure intellectual accomplishment. Unlike traditional systems, CFA does not use colored belts or sashes to identify the student's level of proficiency.

Philosophy

Philosophical resolution is essential to a fighter's mental confidence and clarity. Anyone learning the art of war must find the ultimate answers to questions concerning the use of violence in defense of himself or others. To advance to the highest levels of combat awareness, you must find clear and lucid answers to such provocative questions as could you take the life of another, what are your fears, who are you, why are you interested in studying Contemporary Fighting Arts, why are you reading this book, and what is good and what is evil? If you haven't begun the quest to

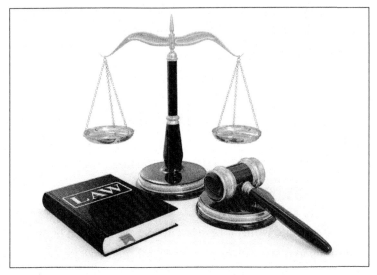

Developing a deadly capability to protect yourself carries tremendous moral and social responsibility. It also involves the risk of civil liability and criminal jeopardy. There is an interesting irony facing most martial artists or self-defense experts. The more highly trained, knowledgeable, and skilled you are in firearms, knives, unarmed combat tactics, martial arts, and other self-defense skills, the higher the standards of care you must follow when protecting yourself and others.

formulate these important questions and answers, then take a break. It's time to figure out just why you want to know the laws and rules of destruction.

Cognitive Combat Skills

Cognitive combat exercises are also important for improving one's fighting skills. CFA uses visualization and crisis rehearsal scenarios to improve general body mechanics, tools and techniques, and maneuvers, as well as tactic selection. Mental clarity, concentration, and emotional control are also developed to enhance one's ability to call upon the controlled killer instinct.

The Spiritual Component

There are many tough fighters out there. In fact, they reside in every town in every country. However, most are nothing more than vicious animals that lack self-mastery. And self-mastery is what separates the true warrior from the eternal novice.

I am not referring to religious precepts or beliefs when I speak of CFA's spiritual component. Unlike most martial arts, CFA does not merge religion into its spiritual aspect. Religion is a very personal and private matter and should never, be incorporated into any fighting system.

CFA's spiritual component is not something that is taught or studied. Rather, it is that which transcends the physical and mental aspects of being and reality. There is a deeper part of each of us that is a tremendous source of truth and accomplishment.

In CFA, the spiritual component is something that is slowly and progressively acquired. During the challenging quest of combat training, one begins to tap the higher qualities of human nature. Those elements of our being that inherently enable us to know right from wrong and good from evil. As we slowly develop this aspect of our total self, we begin to strengthen qualities profoundly important to the "truth." Such qualities are essential to your growth through the mastery of inner peace, the clarity of your "vision," and your recognition of universal truths.

While there are many dedicated individuals who are more than qualified to teach unique philosophical and spiritual components of ancient martial arts, you must realize that such forms of combat can get you killed in a real life self-defense encounter.

One of the goals of my system is to promote virtue and moral responsibility in people who have extreme capacities for physical and mental destructiveness. The spiritual component of fighting is truly the most difficult aspect of personal growth. Yet, unlike the physical component, where the practitioner's abilities will be limited to some degree by genetics and other natural factors, the spiritual component of combat offers unlimited potential for growth and development. In the final analysis, CFA's spiritual component poses the greatest challenges for the student. It is an open-ended plane of unlimited advancement.

The 10 Best Bar Fighting Moves

Chapter One
Before The Brawl..

The 10 Best Bar Fighting Moves

The Elements of Unarmed Combat

In order to benefit from the information discussed in the next chapter, it's important to have a grasp of the following elements of fighting. They are:

- The Fighting Stance
- Fighting Ranges/ Range Proficiency
- Footwork and Mobility
- Combat Attributes
- Natural Body Weapons
- Anatomical Targets
- Probable Reaction Dynamics

The Fighting Stance

The fighting stance defines your ability to execute both explosive punches and defensive techniques, and it will play a material role in the outcome of any fight. It stresses strategic soundness and simplicity over complexity and style. The fighting stance also facilitates optimum execution of your power punches, while simultaneously protecting your vital targets against quick counter strikes.

The fighting stance is designed around the centerline. The centerline is an imaginary vertical line running through the center of the body, from the top of your head to the bottom of the groin. Most of your vital targets are situated along this line, including the head, throat, solar plexus, and groin. Obviously, you want to avoid directly exposing your centerline to the assailant. To achieve this, position your feet and body at a 45-degree angle from the opponent. This moves your body targets back and away from direct strikes but leaves you strategically positioned to attack.

The right lead fighting stance.   *The left lead fighting stance.*

How to Assume a Fighting Stance

When assuming your fighting stance, place your feet about shoulder width apart. Keep your knees bent and flexible. Think of your legs as power springs to launch you through the ranges of unarmed combat (kicking, punching, and grappling range).

Mobility is also important, as we'll discuss later. All footwork and strategic movement should be performed on the balls of your feet. Your weight distribution is also an important factor. Since combat is dynamic, your weight distribution will frequently change. However, when stationary, keep 50 percent of your body weight on each leg and always be in control of it.

The hands are aligned one behind the other along your centerline.

The lead arm is held high and bent at approximately 90 degrees. The rear arm is kept back by the chin. Arranged this way, the hands not only protect the upper centerline but also allow quick deployment of your body weapons. When holding your guard, do not tighten your shoulder or arm muscles prior to striking. Stay relaxed and loose. Finally, keep your chin slightly angled down. This diminishes target size and reduces the likelihood of a paralyzing blow to your chin or a lethal strike to your throat.

A solid fighting stance must be maintained when executing combat techniques. Pictured here, the author (right) maintains the proper hand guard position during the execution of his kick.

The best method for practicing your fighting stance is in front of a full-length mirror. Place the mirror in an area that allows sufficient room for movement; a garage or basement is perfect. Stand in front of the mirror, far enough away to see your entire body. Stand naturally with your arms relaxed at your sides. Now close your eyes and quickly assume your fighting stance. Open your eyes and check for flaws.

Look for low hand guards, improper foot positioning or body angle, rigid shoulders and knees, etc. Drill this way repeatedly, working from both the right and left side. Practice this until your fighting stance becomes second nature.

Fighting Stance Drill (Shadow Fighting)

Shadow fighting is another exercises you can do to improve your fighting stance. Essentially, shadow fighting is the creative deployment of offensive and defensive tools and maneuvers against imaginary assailants from the reference point of a fighting stance.

Shadow fighting requires intense mental concentration, honest self-analysis, and a deep commitment to improve. For those of you on a tight budget, the good news is that shadow fighting is inexpensive. All you need is a full-length mirror and a place to work out. The mirror is vital. It functions as a critic, your personal instructor. If you're honest, the mirror will be too. It will point out every mistake - poor stance structure, telegraphing, sloppy footwork, poor body mechanics, and even lack of physical conditioning.

Proper shadow fighting develops speed, power, balance, footwork, compound attack skills, sound form, and finesse. It even promotes a better understanding of the ranges of combat. As you progress, you can incorporate light dumbbells into shadow fighting workouts to enhance power and speed. Start off with one to three pounds and gradually work your way up. A weight vest can also be worn to develop powerful footwork, kicks, and knee strikes.

If you want to make your fighting stance instinctual, practice it in a slow and controlled fashion with your eyes closed. Closing your eyes when training will help you develop a complete kinesthetic feel for the movement.

The fighting stance is also used as a reference point when training. Here, a student prepares to throw a kick from a fighting stance position.

When shadow fighting be especially aware of the following:

1. Dropping your hands down.

2. Lifting your chin up.

3. Elbows flaring out to the sides.

4. Tensing your muscles before, during and after technique deployment.

5. Unnecessary widening of your feet.

6. Cross stepping when moving sideways.

7. Failing to maintain a 45-degree angle stance.

8. Excessive weight distribution.

The Fighting Ranges and Range Proficiency

Real fighting seldom takes place at a predetermined distance. It can also happen anytime and anywhere. If you want to be prepared to handle any type of combat situation, you'd better be range proficient. Range proficiency is the skill and ability to fight your adversary in all three distances of unarmed combat (kicking range, punching range, and grappling range).

This means that you are capable of fighting an opponent in all possible situations. For example, can you fight an assailant on a bus, in a crowded bar? While lying in your bed or sitting in your car? Do you have the skill to strike an assailant standing five feet away from you? These and other questions pertain to range proficiency.

In unarmed combat, there are only three possible distances from which you can engage your opponent: kicking range, punching range, and grappling range.

Let's start with the kicking range.

Kicking Range

At this distance, you are usually too far to make contact with your hands, so you would use your legs to strike your assailant. For self-defense, you should only employ low-line kicks. These are directed to targets below the assailant's waist, such as the groin, thigh, knee joint, and shin. As a result, I teach my students to use kicking range tools like the vertical, push, side, and hook kicks. They are safe, efficient, and destructive.

The Kicking Range.

Punching Range

This is the midrange of unarmed combat. At this distance, you are close enough to the opponent to strike him with your hands. Hand strikes do not require as much room as kicking, and the surface area that you are standing on is not as crucial a concern.

Effective punching range techniques include the following:: finger jabs, palm heels, knife hands, lead straights, rear crosses, horizontal and shovel hooks, uppercuts, and hammer fists.

The Punching Range.

Grappling Range

The third and closest range of unarmed combat is grappling range. At this distance, you are too close to your opponent to kick or execute some hand strikes, so you would use close-quarter tools and techniques to neutralize your adversary.

Grappling range is divided into two different planes: vertical and horizontal. In the vertical plane, you would deliver impact techniques, some of which include elbow and knee strikes, head butts, gouging and crushing tactics, and biting and tearing techniques.

In the horizontal plane, you are ground fighting with your enemy and can deliver all of the previously mentioned techniques, including various submission holds, locks, and chokes.

Pictured here, vertical grappling range.

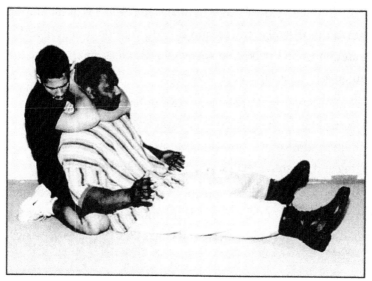

The grappling range (horizontal plane) of unarmed combat. Also known as ground fighting.

Footwork & Mobility

Next are footwork and mobility. I define mobility as the ability to move your body quickly and freely, which is accomplished through basic footwork. The safest footwork involves quick, economical steps performed on the balls of your feet, while you remain relaxed and balanced. Keep in mind that balance is your most important consideration.

Basic footwork can be used for both offensive and defensive purposes, and it is structured around four general directions: forward, backward, right, and left. However, always remember this footwork rule of thumb: Always move the foot closest to the direction you want to go first, and let the other foot follow an equal distance. This prevents cross-stepping, which can cost you your life in a fight.

Basic Footwork Movements

1. Moving forward (advance) - from your fighting stance, first move your front foot forward (approximately 12 inches) and then move your rear foot an equal distance.

2. Moving backward (retreat) - from your fighting stance, first move your rear foot backward (approximately 12 inches) and then move your front foot an equal distance.

3. Moving right (sidestep right) - from your fighting stance, first move your right foot to the right (approximately 12 inches) and then move your left foot an equal distance.

4. Moving left (sidestep left) - from your fighting stance, first move your left foot to the left (approximately 12 inches) and then move your right foot an equal distance.

Practice these four movements for 10 to 15 minutes a day in front of a full-length mirror. In a couple weeks, your footwork should be quick, balanced, and natural.

Circling Right and Left

Strategic circling is an advanced form of footwork where you will use your front leg as a pivot point. This type of movement can also be used defensively to evade an overwhelming assault or to strike the opponent from various strategic angles. Strategic circling can be performed from either a left or right stance.

Circling left (from a left stance) - this means you'll be moving your body around the opponent in a clockwise direction. From a left stance, step 8 to 12 inches to the left with your left foot, then use your left leg as a pivot point and wheel your entire rear leg to the left until the correct stance and positioning is acquired.

Circling right (from a right stance) - from a right stance, step 8 to 12 inches to the right with your right foot, then use your right leg as a pivot point and wheel your entire rear leg to the right until the correct stance and positioning is acquired.

Combat Attributes

A kick, punch, block, or any fighting technique for that matter is useless unless it is accompanied by certain combative attributes. Attributes are qualities that enhance your particular body weapon or technique.

For example, speed, power, timing, non telegraphic movement, rhythm, coordination, accuracy, balance, and range specificity are just a few self-defense attributes that must be present if any technique or maneuver is to be effective in a high-risk self-defense situation.

Let's explore a few basic attributes necessary for fighting: speed, power, timing, balance, and non telegraphic movement.

Speed

To effectively land any offensive strike you must possess speed. By speed, I am referring to how fast your body weapon moves to its target. A fast technique should be likened to the strike of a snake. It should be felt and not seen by your assailant.

While some athletes are blessed with great speed, you should make every possible attempt to develop your speed to the maximum of your ability. One of the easiest ways of enhancing your speed is to simply relax your body prior to executing your body weapon. For example, when executing a palm heel strike to your assailant's chin, your arm should simply shoot straight out and back to its starting point without muscular tension. This may sound simple, but you'd be amazed how many people have difficulty relaxing—especially when they are under tremendous stress. Another way of developing blinding speed is to practice throwing all of your offensive weapons in the air. Focus on quickly executing and retracting your tool or technique as quickly as you can. If you are persistent and work diligently, you can achieve significant results.

Power

Power refers to the amount of impact force you can generate when striking your target. The power of your natural body weapon is not necessarily predicated on your size and strength. A relatively small person can generate devastating power if he or she combines it with sufficient speed. This explains why someone like Bruce Lee who weighed approximately 130 pounds could hit harder than most 200-pound men. Lee knew how to maximize his impact power through the speed at which he executed his techniques.

Ideally, when attempting to strike your assailant, you want to put your entire body behind your blow. I instruct my students to always aim 3 inches through their chosen target. Torquing your hips and shoulder into your blows will also help generate tremendous power. Remember, in a real self-defense situation, you want to hit your assailant with the power equivalent of a shotgun and not a squirt gun.

Timing

Timing refers to your ability to execute a technique or movement at the optimum moment. There are two types of timing: defensive and offensive. Defensive timing is the time between the assailant's attack and your defensive response to that attack. Offensive timing is the time between your recognition of a target opening and your offensive response to that opening.

Among the best ways of developing both offensive and defensive timing are stick and knife fighting, sparring sessions, double-end bag training, and various focus mitt drills. Mental visualization is also another effective method of enhancing timing. Visualizing various self-defense scenarios that require precise timing is ideal for enhancing your skills.

Balance

Effectively striking your assailant requires substantial follow-through while maintaining your balance. Balance is your ability to maintain equilibrium while stationary or moving. You can maintain perfect balance only through controlling your center of gravity, mastering body mechanics, and proper skeletal alignment.

To develop your sense of balance, perform your body weapons and techniques slowly so you become acquainted with the different weight distributions, body positions, and mechanics of each particular weapon. For example, when executing an elbow strike, keep your head, torso, legs, and feet in proper relation to each other. Be certain to follow through your target, but don't overextend yourself.

Non Telegraphic Movement

The element of surprise is an invaluable tool for self-defense. Successfully landing a blow requires that you do not forewarn your assailant of your intentions. Clenching your teeth, widening your eyes, cocking your fist, and tensing your neck or shoulders are just a few common telegraphic cues that will negate the element of surprise.

One of the best ways to prevent telegraphic movement is to maintain a poker face prior to executing your body weapon or technique. Avoid all facial expressions when faced with a threatening assailant. As mentioned, you can study your techniques and maneuvers in front of a full-length mirror or have a friend videotape you performing your movements. These procedures will assist you in identifying and ultimately eliminating telegraphic movements. Be patient and you'll reach your objective.

Natural Body Weapons for Striking

If you want to be able to apply the different fighting methods discussed in the next chapter, you must have a working knowledge of your natural body weapons. Body weapons are simply the various parts of your body that can be used as weapons to neutralize your opponent.

Actually, you have 14 natural body weapons at your immediate disposal. They are easy to learn and, when properly executed, have the potential to disable, cripple, and even kill an attacker. They include the head, teeth, voice, elbows, fists, palms, fingers and nails, edge of hand, web of the hand, knees, shins, dorsum of the foot, heel of foot, and ball of foot.

Let's start with the head.

Head

When you are fighting in close quarters, your head can be used for butting your assailant's nose. Head butts are ideal when a strong attacker has placed you in a hold where your arms are pinned against your sides. Keep in mind that the head butt can be delivered in four different directions: forward, backward, right side, and left side.

Teeth

The teeth can be used for biting anything on the assailant's body (nose, ears, throat, fingers, etc.). It is important, however, for you to muster the mental determination to bite deep and hard into the assailant's flesh and shake your head vigorously, much like a vicious dog killing his enemy. While this may seem primitive and barbaric, it is essential to your survival.

Although a bite is extremely painful, it also transmits a strong psychological message to your assailant. It lets him know that you, too, can be vicious and are willing to do anything to survive the encounter.

Warning: There is one important concern to biting tactics: you run the risk of contracting AIDS if your attacker is infected and you draw blood while biting him.

Elbows

With very little training, you can learn to use your elbows as devastating self-defense weapons. They are explosive, deceptive, and difficult to stop. By rotating your body into the blow, you can generate tremendous force. You can deliver elbow strikes horizontally, vertically, and diagonally to the assailant's nose, temple, chin, throat, solar plexus, and ribs.

Fists

The fists are used for punching an assailant's temple, nose, chin, throat, solar plexus, ribs, and groin. However, punching with your fists is a true art, requiring considerable time and training to master. Punching techniques include the lead straight, rear cross, hooks, upper cuts, shovel hooks, and hammer fists.

Fingers/Nails

Your fingers and nails can be used for jabbing, gouging, and clawing the opponent's eyes. They can also be used for grabbing, pulling, tearing, and crushing his throat or testicles.

Palms

One alternative to punching with your fists is to strike with the heel of your palm. A palm strike from either one of your hands is very powerful and should always be delivered in an upward, thrusting motion to the assailant's nose or chin.

Edge of the Hand

You can throw the edge of your hand in a whiplike motion to surprise and neutralize your attacker. By whipping your arm horizontally to his nose or throat, you can cause severe injury or death. The edge of your hand can also be thrown vertically or diagonally to the back of the assailant's neck as a finishing blow.

Web of the Hand

The web of your hand can be used to deliver web hand strikes to the opponent's throat. When striking, be certain to keep your hand stiff with your palm facing down.

Knees

When you are fighting the opponent in close-quarter grappling range, your knees can be extremely powerful weapons. You can deliver knee strikes vertically and diagonally to the assailant's thigh and groin, ribs, solar plexus, and face.

Shins

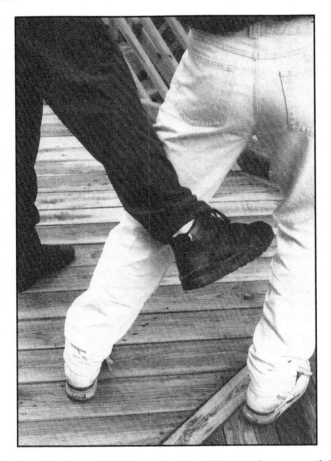

Striking with your shinbone can quickly cripple a powerful assailant and bring him to his knees in agony. That's right—your shinbone is a weapon. When striking with your shin, you can aim for his thigh, the side of his knee, or groin—and always remember to aim through your target.

Dorsum of Foot

You can use the dorsum of your foot to execute a vertical kick to the assailant's groin, and in some cases, his head. Striking with the dorsum increases the power of your kick, prevents broken toes, and also lengthens the surface area of your strike.

Heel of Foot

You can use the heel of your foot to execute a side kick to the opponent's knee or shin. When fighting an attacker in grappling range, you can use the heel of your foot to stomp down on the assailant's instep or toes.

Ball of Foot

You can use the ball of your foot to execute a push kick into the assailant's thigh. You can also snap it quickly into the assailant's shin to loosen a grab from the front. When striking the assailant with the ball of your foot, be certain to pull your toes back to avoid jamming or breaking them.

Anatomical Targets

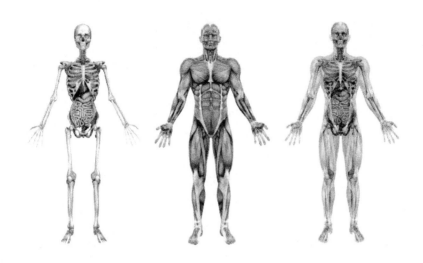

Knowing how and when to strike your opponent is essential; however knowing where to hit him is equally important. Anyone who is seriously interested in neutralizing a formidable adversary must have a working knowledge and understanding of the body targets on the human anatomy. This is called target orientation.

Many people don't realize that the human body has many structural weaknesses that are especially vulnerable to attack. The human body simply was not designed to take the punishment of strikes and blows. Always keep in mind that regardless of your attacker's size, strength, or state of mind, he will always have vulnerable targets that can be attacked.

Unfortunately, very little information has been written on anatomical targets and the medical implications of self-defense strikes. Every martial artist, self-defense expert, combat specialist, and law enforcement officer has a moral and legal responsibility to know the medical implications of strikes and techniques. It is your responsibility to know which targets will stun, incapacitate, disfigure, cripple, or kill your assailant. Knowledge of the medical implications will also make you a more efficient technician.

I am astonished by some martial art and self-defense instructors who teach ineffective targets. For example, the biceps, collar bone, kidneys, coronal suture, or Achilles tendon are just a few targets that yield poor results when struck. Such anatomical targets won't neutralize a vicious opponent immediately. In many cases, it will only anger him and provoke him to attack with greater viciousness and determination. Therefore, it is essential that you strike targets that will immediately incapacitate the opponent. Anything less can get you severely injured or killed. Don't forget this point.

For practical purposes you only need to know a handful of anatomical targets. We will focus on 13 vulnerable targets categorized into three zones.

The 3 Target Zones

For reasons of clarity, we can categorize both the primary and secondary anatomical targets into one of three possible zones.

Zone 1 (Head region) consists of targets related to your senses. This includes: the eyes, temples, nose, chin, and back of neck.

Zone 2 (Neck, Torso, Groin) consists of targets related to breathing. This includes: the throat, solar plexus, ribs, and testicles.

Zone 3 (Legs, Feet) consists of targets related to mobility. This includes: the thighs, knees, shins, instep, and toes.

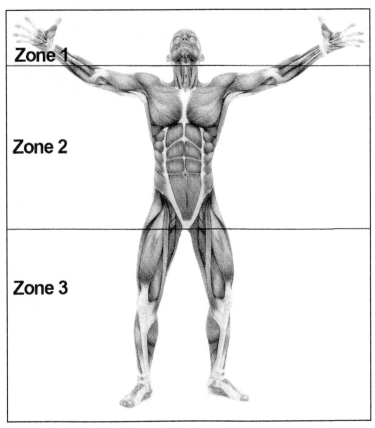

The three target zones.

EYES

Eyes sit in the orbital bones of the skull. They are ideal targets for self-defense because they are extremely sensitive and difficult to protect, and striking them requires very little force. The eyes can be poked, scratched,  and gouged from a variety of angles. Depending on the force of your strike, it can cause numerous injuries, including watering of the eyes, hemorrhaging, blurred vision, temporary or permanent blindness, severe pain, rupture, shock, and unconsciousness.

NOSE

The nose is made up of a thin bone, cartilage, numerous blood vessels, and many nerves. It is a particularly good target because it stands out from the opponent's face and can be struck from three different directions (up, straight, down). A moderate blow can cause stunning pain, eye-watering, temporary blindness, and hemorrhaging. A powerful strike can result in shock and unconsciousness.

CHIN

In boxing, the chin is considered a "knockout button," responsible for retiring hundreds of boxers. The chin is equally a good target for self-defense. When it is struck at a 45-degree angle, shock is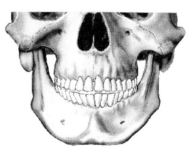

transmitted to the cerebellum and cerebral hemispheres of the brain, resulting in paralysis and immediate unconsciousness. Other possible injuries include broken jaw, concussion, and whiplash to the neck.

TEMPLE

The temple or sphenoid bone is a thin, weak bone located on the side of the skull approximately 1 inch from the eyes. Because of its fragile structure and close proximity to the brain, a powerful strike to this target can be deadly. Other injuries include unconsciousness, hemorrhage, concussion, shock, and coma.

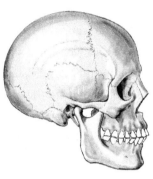

THROAT

The throat is a lethal target because it is only protected by a thin layer of skin. This region consists of the thyroid, hyaline and crocoid cartilage, trachea, and larynx. The trachea, or windpipe, is a cartilaginous tube that measures 4 1/2 inches in length and is approximately 1 inch in diameter. A

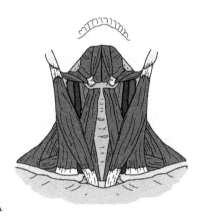

powerful strike to this target can result in unconsciousness, blood drowning, massive hemorrhaging, air starvation, and death. If the thyroid cartilage is crushed, hemorrhaging will occur, the windpipe will quickly swell shut, resulting in suffocation.

GROIN

Everyone man will agree that the genitals are highly sensitive organs. Even a light strike can be debilitating. A moderate strike to the groin can result in severe pain, nausea, vomiting, shortness of breath, and possible sterility. A powerful blow to the groin can crush the scrotum and testes against the pubic bones, causing shock and unconsciousness.

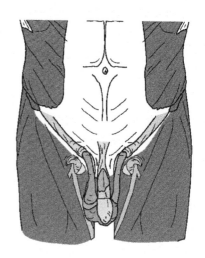

THIGHS

Many people don't realize that the thighs are also vulnerable targets. A moderate kick to the rectus femoris or vastus lateralis muscles will result in immediate immobility of the leg. An extremely hard kick to the thigh can result in a fracture of the femur, resulting in internal bleeding, severe pain, cramping, and immobility of the broken leg.

BACK OF NECK

The back of the neck consists of the first seven vertebrae of the spinal column. They act as a circuit board for nerve impulses from the brain to the body. The back of the neck is a lethal target because the vertebrae are poorly protected. A very powerful strike to the back of the neck can cause shock,

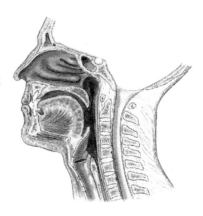

unconsciousness, a broken neck, complete paralysis, coma, and death.

RIBS

There are 12 pair of ribs in the human body. Excluding the eleventh and twelfth ribs, they are long and slender bones that are joined by the vertebral column in the back and the sternum and costal cartilage in the front.

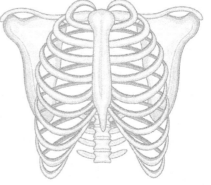

Since there are no eleventh and twelfth ribs (floating ribs) in the front, you should direct your strikes to the ninth and tenth ribs. A moderate strike to the anterior region of the ribs will cause severe pain and shortness of breath. A powerful 45-degree blow could easily break a rib and force it into a lung, resulting in its collapse, internal hemorrhaging, severe pain, air starvation, unconsciousness, and possible death.

SOLAR PLEXUS

The solar plexus is a large
collection of nerves situated below
the sternum in the upper abdomen.
A moderate blow to this area will
cause nausea, tremendous pain,
and shock, making it difficult for
the assailant to breathe. A powerful
strike to the solar plexus can result
in severe abdominal pain and
cramping, air starvation, and shock.

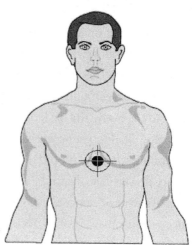

KNEES

The knee connects the femur to the
tibia. It is a very weak joint held together by
a number of supporting ligaments. When
the assailant's leg is locked or fixed and a
forceful strike is delivered to the front of
the joint, the cruciate ligaments will tear,
resulting in excruciating pain, swelling, and
immobility.

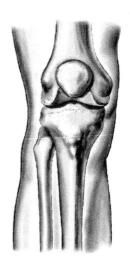

Located on the front of the knee joint is
the patella, which is made of a small, loose
piece of bone. The patella is also extremely
vulnerable to dislocation by a direct,
forceful kick. Severe pain, swelling, and
immobility will quickly result.

SHINS

Everyone, at one time or another, has knocked his or her shin bone into the end of a table or bed accidentally and felt the intense pain associated with it. The shin is very sensitive because the bone is only protected by a thin layer of skin. However, a powerful kick delivered to this target can easily fracture it, resulting in nauseating pain, hemorrhaging, and immobility.

FINGERS

The fingers or digits are considered weak and vulnerable targets that can easily be jammed, sprained, broken, torn, and bitten. While a broken finger might not stop an attacker, it will certainly make him release his hold. A broken finger also makes it difficult for the assailant to clench his fist or hold a weapon. When attempting to break an assailant's finger, it's best to grab the pinkie and forcefully tear backward against the knuckle.

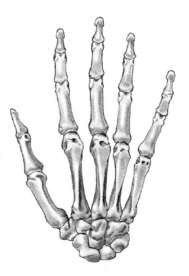

TOES/INSTEP

With a powerful stomp of your heel, you can break the small bones of an assailant's toes and or instep, causing severe pain and immobility. Stomping on the toes is an excellent technique for releasing many holds. It should be mentioned, however, that you should avoid an attack to the toes/instep if the attacker is wearing hard leather boots, i.e., combat, hiking, or motorcycle boots.

Probable Reaction Dynamics (PRD)

In my book, *Maximum Damage: Hidden Secrets Behind Brutal Fighting Combinations*, I define probable reaction dynamics as the opponent's anticipated or predicted movements or actions that occur in both armed and unarmed combat. Probable reaction dynamics will always be the result or residual of your initial action, i.e., kick, punch, etc.

The most basic example of probable reaction dynamics can be illustrated by the following scenario. Let's say, you deliver a powerful kick to the opponent's groin. When your foot comes in contact with its target, your opponent will exhibit one of several *possible* physical or psychological reactions to your strike. These responses might include:

- The opponent's head and body violently drop forward.

- The opponent grabs or covers his groin region.

- The opponent struggles for breath.

- The opponent momentarily freezes.

- The opponent goes into shock.

Knowledge of your assailant's probable reaction dynamics is vital in all forms of combat, especially when it comes to bar fighting. In fact, you must be mindful of the possible reaction dynamics to every strike, and technique in your arsenal. This is exactly what I refer to as *"reaction dynamic awareness"* and I can assure you this is not such an easy task. However, with regular training, it can be developed.

Just remember, understanding and ultimately mastering reaction dynamic awareness will give you a tremendous advantage in a fight by maximizing the effectiveness, efficiency and safety of your compound attack.

Flow Like Water!

When you proceed with the compound attack, always maintain the offensive flow. The offensive flow is a progression of continuous offensive movements designed to neutralize or, in some cases, terminate your adversary. The key is to have each strike flow smoothly and efficiently from one to the next without causing you to lose ground. Subjecting your adversary to an offensive flow is especially effective because it taxes his nervous system, thereby dramatically lengthening his defensive reaction time.

In a real-life emergency situation it's critical that you always keep the offensive pressure on until your opponent is completely neutralized. Always remember that letting your offensive flow stagnate, even for a second, will open you up to numerous dangers and risks.

Proper breathing is another substantial element of the compound attack, and there is one simple rule that should be followed: exhale during the execution phase of your kick or strike and inhale during its retraction phase. Above all, never hold your breath when delivering several consecutive blows. Doing so could lead to dizziness and fainting, among other complications.

You Don't Have Much Time

Your body can only sustain delivering a compound attack for so long. Initially, your brain will quickly release adrenaline into your blood stream, which will fuel your fighting and enhance your strength and power. This lethal boost of energy is known as an adrenaline dump. However, your ability to exert and maintain this maximum effort will last no more than 30 to 60 seconds if you are in above-average shape. If the fight continues after that, your strength and speed may drop by as much as 50 percent below normal. When all is said and done, you don't have much time in a fight, so the battle needs to be won fast before your energy runs out!

Don't Forget To Relocate!

Subsequent to your compound attack, immediately move to a new location by flanking your adversary. This tactic is known as relocating. Based on the principles of strategy, movement, and surprise, relocating dramatically enhances your safety by making it difficult for your adversary to identify your position after you have attacked him. Remember, if your opponent doesn't know exactly where you are, he won't be able to effectively counterattack.

Actuate Recovery Breathing

Implementing an explosive compound attack will often leave you winded. Because of the volatile nature of street combat, even highly conditioned fighters will show signs of oxygen debt. Hence it's important to employ recovery breathing, the active process of quickly restoring your breathing to its normal state. It requires taking long, deep breaths in a controlled rhythm while avoiding rapid, short gasping. Wind sprints are great for improving your recovery breathing. Consider adding them to your regular training program.

The 10 Best Bar Fighting Moves

Chapter Two
The Ten Best Bar Fighting Moves

The 10 Best Bar Fighting Moves

The Ten Best Bar Fighting Moves

In this chapter, I'm going to teach you ten of my best bar fighting moves. Keep in mind that every bar fight will be different and not every tactical tactic or technique is going to be ideal for your particular circumstance. It will be up to you to decide which one best suits your situation. Remember to always use your best judgment and never use physical force against another person unless it's morally and legally justified in the eyes of the law.

1. Know What The Hell is Going On Around You

Situational awareness is total alertness, presence, and focus on virtually everything in your immediate surroundings. You must train your senses to detect and assess the people, places, objects, and actions that can pose a danger to you. Do not think of situational awareness simply in terms of the five customary senses of sight, sound, smell, taste, and touch. In addition, the very real powers of instinct and intuition must also be developed and eventually relied upon.

Two vagrants congregating on the street corner or by your car, the stranger lingering at the mailboxes in your lobby, the delivery man at the door, a deserted parking lot, an alleyway near a familiar sidewalk, the loudmouth drunk staring you down from the end of the bar... these are all obvious examples of persons, places, and objects that can pose a threat to you. Situational awareness need not - and should not - be limited to preconceived notions about obvious sources of danger.

Unfortunately, very few people have refined their situational awareness skills. The reasons are many. Some are in denial about the prevalence of criminal violence while others are too distracted by life's everyday problems and pressures to pay attention to the hidden dangers that lurk around them. Whatever the reasons, poor awareness skills can get you into serious trouble and could cost you your life.

Situational awareness requires you to train your senses to detect and assess the people, places, objects, and actions that can pose a danger to you.

Situational awareness, in terms of threats posed by human attackers, begins with an understanding of criminal psychology. It is a common misconception that criminals are stupid and incompetent. Although many may be uneducated by traditional standards, they are not stupid. On the contrary, they can be shrewd, methodical, bold, and psychologically dominant. The especially dangerous ones are often expert observers of human behavior, capable of accurately assessing your body language, walk, talk, carriage, state of mind, and a variety of other indicators. They know what to look for and how to exploit it.

Chapter Two: The 10 Best Bar Fighting Moves

Criminals are also selective predators. Many rapists, for example, will test a victim by engaging her in idle conversation, following her, or invading her space in some preliminary and seemingly harmless manner. Carefully selected measures designed to evaluate fear, apprehension, and awareness are part of the attacker's overall strategy. Seasoned criminal aggressors are looking for easy strikes - what they call the "vic." Chronic barroom brawlers, street punks, and muggers operate in the same basic manner. They look for the weak, timid, disoriented, and unaware victims.

As you develop situational awareness, you transmit a different kind of signal to the enemy's radar. Weakness and uncertainty are replaced by confidence and strength. Your carriage and movements change. You will be seen as assertive and purposeful. You are less likely to be perceived as an easy mark or a "vic," and your chances of being attacked will significantly diminish.

Situational awareness also diminishes the potency of the criminal's favorite weapon—surprise. Your ability to foresee and detect danger will diminish his ability to stalk you, or lie in wait in ambush zones.

Ambush zones are strategic locations from which criminal assailants launch their attacks. Every day millions of Americans walk through numerous ambush zones and never even know it. Ambush zones are everywhere. They can be found and exploited in unfamiliar and familiar environments, even in your home, and in unpopulated and populated areas. An ambush zone can be set in a dark or poorly lit area as well as in a well-lit area. An ambush zone can be established in a variety of common places: under, behind, or around trees, utility boxes, shrubs, beds, corners, dumpsters, doorways, walls, tables, cars, trash cans, rooftops, bridges, ramps, mailboxes, etc. They are everywhere!

How many ambush zones are in this photo?

In addition to enhancing your ability to detect, avoid, and strategically neutralize ambush zones, situational awareness allows you to detect and avoid threats and dangers not necessarily predicated on the element of surprise. Some situations afford potential victims the luxury of actually seeing trouble coming. Nonetheless, it's remarkable how many people fail to heed obvious signs of danger because of poor awareness skills. They overlook the signals—belligerence, furtiveness, hostility, restlessness—so often manifested by criminal attackers. They neglect the opportunity to cross the street long before the shoulder-to-shoulder encounter with a pack of young toughs moving up the sidewalk. Once it's too late to avoid the confrontation, a whole new range of principles comes quickly into play. The best defense is a heightened level of situational awareness. You must learn to avoid situations that will require the use of physical force, and the highest form of self-defense is being smart enough to avoid the encounter in the first place.

Situational Awareness Exercises

- Detect five different ambush zones at your workplace and write them down. Don't pick the obvious ones. It's your life; learn to think like a bad guy.

- Detect five different ambush zones in some of the bars you frequently visit. If you didn't find five, you didn't look hard enough.

- Over the next ten days do not allow yourself to be taken by surprise - by anyone! Every time it happens, record the circumstances: who, what, when, how, where, and why.

- When you watch television, go to the movies, look at pictures, or read books, note ambush zones that have not occurred to you in your other assessments. Note them in writing.

- Visualize five different settings. They can be friendly and familiar like your backyard, or hostile and strange. Write down the things that you have mentally noted in these visualized settings.

2. Listen to Your Five Senses

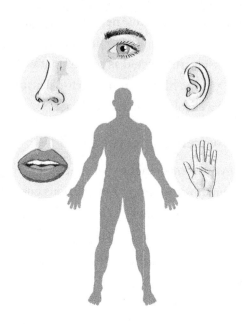

We assess many different things every day. For example, we assess such divergent things as shopping values, the pros and cons of career moves, and different aspects of our relationships with others. The requisite skills for these assessments vary, depending on the elements involved. Skills for assessing the effect of fluctuating interest rates on the stock market are very different from those necessary to assess the effect of a volcano on global weather patterns. The analytical processes may be similar, but the knowledge and skills need to be encountered individually, and not arbitrarily.

Similarly, in the world of self-defense, threat assessment is the process of rapidly gathering and analyzing information, then accurately evaluating it in terms of threat and danger. In general, you can assess people, places, objects, and actions. In addition, assessment skills require sharp perception and keen observation. Your perception skills can be heightened, and your ability to observe can be enhanced.

We gather information through our sensory processes. You see a movement in the shadows of your backyard. You hear footsteps approaching from behind you in a dark parking lot. You smell cigarette smoke in what you thought was a deserted area. You feel a breeze coming up your stairwell when all the doors and windows are supposed to be shut. You taste the sickening metallic flavor of fear in your mouth.

These five senses can be sharpened through a variety of exercises designed to develop both raw detection and learned identification capabilities. For example, sit alone in your backyard for a given period of time and catalog the various things your five senses detect. Next, list the possible sources of the sensory data. With practice, you will make remarkable progress from being unable to detect a particular sound or smell to not only detecting it quickly and accurately but also identifying its source. This development increases as these exercises are performed in different types of settings. Imagine, for example, the things you would hear, see, and smell on a dark night in the middle of a suburban park, as opposed to what you would experience standing in a dark urban alley. Remember, you are only limited by your imagination.

Additionally, you can also heighten your ability to observe. Have you ever noticed how keenly you study people, buildings, streets, signs, animals, and various other everyday things when you travel to a strange city or to another country? Watch a dog in a new environment, with its nose in the air and ears perked in alertness. People and animals tend to observe more actively in strange or new environments. This practice reveals an old survival process at work. Conversely, we tend to become less observant in familiar settings. We let our guard down, so to speak. For example, how many times has your wife or girlfriend changed her hair, or your husband or boyfriend shaved his beard, and you simply didn't notice it?

Here's the good news: observational skills can be expanded with application of an intelligent program. In my Contemporary Fighting Arts (CFA) self-defense system, students are instructed to practice quickly, memorizing lines of verse in a hectic setting. The turmoil around them can work to strengthen their concentration. In some situations students will practice studying scenes on the streets, trying to spot the threat or potential danger. It might be a suspicious man lurking in an alleyway, a group of restless youths congregating at a street corner, or a figure in a second-story window cradling what might be a high-powered rifle. These are just a few exercises to sharpen your self-defense and observational skills. Military and intelligence agencies are experts in this area of training.

Even though the senses can be sharpened and the powers of observation enhanced, the ability to process information varies with the individual. Two average untrained people who witness the same event are likely to report it differently. This is referred to as "individual perception." In part, previous experiences can determine the manner in which an individual will react to stimuli. People of different ages, cultures, or occupational backgrounds may see the same event very differently. The actual physical processes involved in perception are much the same in every person. But it is the manner in which data is interpreted that determines what a person sees. When it comes to self-defense, you must attempt to remove preconceived notions, assumptions, and biases that may lead to dangerously incorrect conclusions or oversights. These false reactions form actual blocks to your ability to grasp reality.

3. Choose The Right Move

Accurate assessment is critical in self-defense for two reasons. First, it is imperative that you choose the most appropriate tactical response. There are five possible tactical responses to any particular self-defense situation, listed in order of increasing level of resistance:

- Comply
- Escape
- De-escalate
- Assert
- Fight Back

Accurate assessment skills will help you choose the appropriate response for the situation.

COMPLY

Comply means to obey the assailant's commands. For example, if you are held at gun point (out of disarming range) for the purpose of robbery, there is nothing to do but comply. Take out your wallet, take off your watch, hand over your car keys, do what you are told. Comply.

ESCAPE

Escape means to flee from the threat or danger safely and rapidly. For example, if you are being held hostage and your captor is distracted long enough for you to escape safely, then do it.

DE-ESCALATE

De-escalate means the art and science of diffusing a hostile individual. Not every confrontation warrants fighting back. Often you will be able to use de-escalation skills to talk someone out of a possible violent encounter. An intoxicated loudmouth at the bar may be just the type of guy you can settle down and lead away from a problem with effective de-escalation skills. (I'll discuss more of this later.)

ASSERT

Assert means standing up for you and your rights. Through effective communication skills you can thwart a person's efforts to intimidate, dominate, and control you. For example, let's say you're working late at the office and your boss makes sexual advances toward you. Now is the time to confront him and be assertive. In a firm and confidant manner, you tell him that you're not interested and that you want him to stop his offensive actions immediately.

FIGHT BACK

Fight back means using various physical and psychological tactics and techniques to stun, incapacitate, cripple or kill your attacker(s). For example, you're trapped in a dead-end alley by a knife-wielding psychotic who appears determined to butcher you. Your only option is to fight back!

Tactical options are fluid and can change from one moment to the next.

Chapter Two: The 10 Best Bar Fighting Moves

These are just a few of the many possible examples of the five tactical responses. Every self-defense situation is different, and, moreover, most situations can be fluid. A dangerous situation might present an escape option at one moment but quickly turn into a fight-back situation at the next. For example, let's say that you are kidnapped and your captor leaves a door unlocked, and in your effort to escape, you run into him on your way out. Obviously, that is the time to fight for your life.

There is a second important reason why assessment skills are critical in self-defense: the law. There is an interesting irony facing all law enforcement officers, self-defense, and martial art experts. The more highly trained, knowledgeable, and better you are in firearms, knives, combat tactics, martial arts, and other self-defense skills, the higher the standard of care you must observe when protecting yourself or others. If you act too quickly or use what someone might consider "excessive force" in neutralizing an assailant, you may end up being a defendant in a legal process.

America is the most violent society on earth. It is also the most litigious. Most people do not realize that developing a deadly capability to protect yourself carries a tremendous moral and social responsibility. It also involves the risk of civil liability and criminal jeopardy. If you blind or cripple a person, you'd better be prepared to justify this act in the eyes of the law. If you're not careful, you could spend the rest of your life supporting the person who meant to harm you - assuming, of course, that you can get a job once you get out of jail!

The two most popular questions students ask after they have had a little self-defense training are when can you use physical force, and how much physical force is justified? Well, there are no simple answers to these questions. Again, every self-defense situation is different. In one case, a side kick that dislocates an attacker's knee might be judged appropriate force. Change the facts a little and you have a civil battery suit and a criminal charge of aggravated assault. Killing a criminal attacker in one situation may be justified, but a seemingly similar case might result in a civil suit for wrongful death and a criminal charge of manslaughter or murder.

The basic principle is that you must never use force against another person unless it is justified. For civilians, force is broken down into two broad categories: lethal and nonlethal. Any time you use physical force against another person, you run the risk of having a civil suit filed against you. Anyone can hire a lawyer and file a suit for damages. Likewise, anyone can file a criminal complaint against you. Whether criminal charges will be brought against you depends upon the prosecutor or grand jury's views of the facts. No two cases are the same, so there are no easy answers.

Most people do not realize that developing a deadly capability to protect yourself carries a tremendous moral and social responsibility. It also involves the risk of civil liability and criminal jeopardy.

I am not qualified to be offering you legal advice. Frankly, I know enough about the law not to make that mistake. However, I can tell you that if you are a highly trained self-defense expert, you will be held to a higher standard of behavior by a jury of your peers. Now there's a good one for you - a jury of your peers. If I ever have to be on trial, I hope that the jury will be comprised of twelve trained self-defense experts. But I won't hold my breath.

A particular troublesome angle to self-defense and legal liability is my first-strike principle (I'll discuss more of this later on). In many cases, jurors will decide self-defense issues on who struck whom first. That's not good news. My rule is: when faced with a harmful or deadly force situation, and when danger is imminent, then strike first, strike fast, and strike with authority.

The problem arises because you may have a hard time justifying your approach in the antiseptic and safe environment of a courtroom many months later. Whenever my life has been in imminent danger, I always acted swiftly. Whether you adopt this approach is entirely up to you.

4. Know What to Assess

You should always be alert. Don't become complacent and comfortable. Never assume there is no danger! Learn to assess the situation promptly and accurately, reach a rational conclusion, and choose the appropriate tactical response. The only time you should forget about assessment is when you've been attacked by surprise. For example, a drunkard from behind, grabs you by the neck, and throws you to the ground. Then it's too late for assessment skills. You must act intuitively and immediately to neutralize him, or you're going to be a statistic. Remember, time is of the essence, and your reaction and reflex must take the place of assessment.

What to Assess

There are two broad factors to assess in any self-defense situation: the environment and the individual(s). Let's first look at the environment and its related factors.

The Environment

In any self-defense situation you must strategically evaluate your environment, which is made up of your immediate surroundings. It can be a parking lot, your car, your bedroom, your office, an airport, a park, elevator, bar, movie theater, etc. There are four essential factors to consider when assessing your environment. They are escape routes, barriers, makeshift weapons, and terrain. Let's take a look at each one.

ESCAPE ROUTES

These are the various avenues or exits from a threatening situation. There is nothing cowardly about running away from a dangerous situation. The ultimate goal of self-defense is to survive. Some possible escape routes are windows, doors, fire escapes, gates, escalators, fences, walls, bridges, and staircases. But be careful that your version of an escape route doesn't lead you into a worse situation.

BARRIERS

A barrier is any object that obstructs the attacker's path of attack. At the very least, barriers give you distance and some precious time, and they may give you some safety—at least temporarily. A barrier must have the structural integrity to perform the particular function you have assigned it. Barriers are everywhere and include such things as large desks, doors, automobiles, Dumpsters, large trees, fences, walls, heavy machinery, and large vending machines. The list is endless and depends on the situation, but it is a good idea to assess in advance any possible barriers when entering a potentially hostile or dangerous environment.

MAKESHIFT WEAPONS

These are common, everyday objects that can be converted into offensive and defensive weapons. Like a barrier, a makeshift weapon must be appropriate to the function you have assigned to it. You won't be able to knock someone out with a car antennae, but you could whip it across their eyes and temporarily blind them. Whereas you could knock someone unconscious with a good heavy flashlight but you could not use it to shield yourself from a knife attack.

Makeshift weapons can be broken down into four types: striking, distracting, shielding, and cutting weapons.

Striking makeshift weapons, as the name implies, are objects that can be used to strike an assailant. Examples include heavy flashlights, baseball bats, bottles, beer mugs, text books, binoculars, small lamps, hammers, pool cues, canes, umbrellas, vases, walking sticks, crowbars, light dumbbells, barstools, chairs, etc.

Distracting makeshift weapons are objects that can be thrown at the attacker(s) to temporarily distract him. Depending on the size of the object, a distraction weapon can be thrown into an assailant's face, body, or legs. They include car keys, glass bottles, rolled-up newspaper or magazine, text books, dirt, gravel, sand, hot liquids, spare change, ashtrays, paperweights, wallets, purses, and briefcases. Trash cans, chairs, and bicycles can also be kicked or slammed into an assailant's legs.

Shielding makeshift weapons are objects that temporarily shield you from the assailant's punch, kick, or strike. In some cases, shielding weapons can also be used to protect against knife and bludgeon attacks. Examples of shielding weapons include: trash can lids, briefcases, luggage bags, doors, sofa cushions, thick pillows, ironing boards, hubcaps, food trays, lawn chairs, small tables, backpack, etc.

Cutting makeshift weapons are objects that can be used to cut the assailant by either stabbing or slashing him. Examples include all kitchen cutlery, forks, screwdrivers, broken bottles, broken glass, scissors, car keys, pitch forks, ice scrapers, letter openers, pens, sharp pencils, razor blades, etc. Obviously there is some overlap between the various categories of make-shift weapons. For example, a briefcase can be thrown into an attacker's face for distraction, used to shield against a knife attack, or slammed into an assailant's temple to knock him out.

TERRAIN

This is a critical environmental factor. What are the strategic implications of the terrain that you are standing on? Will the surface area interfere with your ability to defend against an assailant? Is the terrain wet or dry, mobile or stationary? Obviously, if you are standing on ice, you will be restricted in your efforts to quickly escape or attempt kicking techniques. If the surface is shaky, like a suspension bridge, for example, you may be required to avoid kicking your assailant and instead fight back with hand techniques.

The Individual(s)

Obviously, in a potentially dangerous situation, you need to assess the source of the threat. Who is posing the possible danger? Is it someone you know or is he a complete stranger? Is it one person or two or more? What are his or her intentions in confronting you? Pay attention to all available clues, particularly verbal and nonverbal indicators. Let all five of your senses go to work to absorb the necessary information. Also don't forget to listen to what your gut instincts are telling you about the threatening person(s). There are five essential factors to consider when assessing a threatening individual: demeanor, intent, range, positioning, and weapon capability.

DEMEANOR

In the broadest terms we are talking about the individual's outward behavior. Watch for clues and cues. Is he shaking, or is he calm and calculated? Are his shoulders hunched or relaxed? Are his hands clenched? Is his neck taut? Are his teeth clenched? Is he breathing hard? Does he seem angry or frustrated, or confused and scared? Does he seem high on drugs? Is he mentally ill or simply intoxicated? What is he saying? How is he saying it? Is his speech slurred? What is his tone of voice? Is he talking rapidly or methodically? Is he cursing and angry? All of these verbal and nonverbal cues are essential in assessing the individual's overall demeanor and thus adjusting your tactical response accordingly.

INTENT

Once you've got a good read on the assailant's demeanor, you're in a much better position to assess his or her intent. In other words, just what is this person's purpose in confronting you? Does he intend to rob you? Is he seeking retribution for something you have done? Or is he simply looking to pick a fight with you? Determining the individual's intent is perhaps the most important assessment factor, but it can also be the most difficult. Moreover, when it comes to criminal intent, things can change pretty quickly. For example, an intent to rob can quickly turn into an intent to rape. In any event, the appropriate tactical response is highly dependent upon a correct assessment of intent.

RANGE OR DISTANCE

"Range" is the spatial relationship between you and the assailant(s) in terms of distance. In self-defense there are three possible distances from which your assailant can launch an attack: Kicking range, Punching range, and Grappling range.

Kicking range is the furthest range from which the attacker can kick you, lunge at you with or without a weapon, or strike you with a bludgeon.

The kicking range.

Punching range is the midrange from which the attacker can strike you with his hands, grab or push you, cut you with a knife, or strike you with a bludgeon.

Punching range.

Grappling range is the closest range, from which the assailant can wrestle, grab, push, or choke you, and cut you with an edged weapon.

Grappling range.

The 10 Best Bar Fighting Moves

When assessing a threatening individual, you'll need to recognize the strategic implications of his range. For example, how close is he from launching a punch? Is he at a distance from which he could kick you? Is he in a range that allows him to grab hold of you, take you to the ground, or cut you with an edged weapon? Is he moving through the ranges of unarmed combat? If so, how fast? Does he continue to move forward when you step back?

POSITIONING

This is the spatial relationship of the assailant(s) to you in terms of threat, escape, and target selection. Are you surrounded by multiple assailants or only one? Is he standing squarely or sideways, above or below you? What anatomical targets does the assailant present you with? Is he blocking the door or any other avenue of escape? Is his back to the light source? Is he close to your only makeshift weapon? You must answer these questions before choosing a tactical strategy appropriate to the situation.

WEAPON CAPABILITY

Is your assailant armed or unarmed? If he is carrying a weapon, what type is it? Does he have a delivery method for the particular weapon? Is he armed with more than one weapon? Sometimes it is easy to determine if someone is armed. For example, you see a knife sheath on his belt. At other times your assessment skills need to be more advanced. For example, is the person wearing a jacket when it is too hot for a jacket? Could it be to conceal a gun at the waist? Is the person patting his chest? When scanning the person, can you see his hands and all his fingertips? Is one hand behind him or in his pockets? Could he be palming a knife or some other edged weapon? Are his arms crossed? Does he seem to be reaching for something?

Does he seem suspiciously rooted to a particular spot? Is his body language incongruous with his verbal cues you are reading? The CFA rule: When you're not certain, always assume your assailant is armed with a weapon.

Just because you can't see it, doesn't mean it's not there.

5. Master De-escalation Skills

One thing that will separate you from every other Joe Schmo that walks into a bar is the ability to a de-escalate and strategically diffuse a hostile person. But what is de-escalation and why is it important for bar fighting?

De-escalation is the strategic process of diffusing a potentially violent confrontation. The goal is to eliminate the possibility of an agitated individual resorting to physical violence. In my

The 10 Best Bar Fighting Moves

Contemporary Fight Arts fighting system, de-escalation is a delicate mixture of science and art, psychology and warfare. It requires you to use both verbal and nonverbal techniques to calm the hostile person, while employing tactically deceptive physical safeguards to create the appearance that you are totally non aggressive. It is the art of "tactically calming" the aggressor. You must be in total control of yourself, both physically and emotionally in order to deal effectively with someone on the verge of losing control. By mastering my de-escalation stance, you will greatly enhance your capability to diffuse the escalating dynamics of a hostile confrontation.

In all my years of teaching and training in the martial sciences and self-defense, I have noticed that most systems of self-defense overlook the importance of de-escalation skills. It is sometimes tragically ironic that in many martial art styles years are spent on developing and perfecting fighting skills, but little or no time is spent on the knowledge and skills necessary to diffuse a potentially violent encounter. It is discouraging indeed that so many martial artists fail to grasp or don't even bother trying to understand the psychological and emotional aspects of human aggression and conflict.

De-escalation Stance Characteristics

The de-escalation stance is used exclusively during the pre-contact stage of bar fighting and there are two variations that you will need to master. They are:

- De-escalation Stance (kicking & punching range)
- De-escalation Stance (grappling range)
- De-escalation Stance (kicking & punching range)

This stance is used when you are facing an opponent in either the kicking or punching range of unarmed combat.

When assuming this de-escalation stance, keep your head straight and focused directly at your adversary. Like the fighting stance, you should keep your chin slightly angled down. This diminishes target size and reduces the likelihood of a paralyzing blow to the chin or a lethal strike to the throat. However, it's very important that you appear nonthreatening and non combative to your adversary.

The centerline of your torso should be strategically positioned at a 45-degree angle from your adversary. When assuming the

HANDS
STAGGERED
FORMATION

HANDS
OPEN &
RELAXED

TORSO
BLADED

ELBOWS
TUCKED
IN

KNEES
BENT

FEET
SHOULDER-WIDTH
APART

FEET
PARALLEL

The de-escalation stance for kicking and punching distance.

The 10 Best Bar Fighting Moves

de-escalation stance, place your strongest, most coordinated side forward. For example, a right-handed person stands with his or her right side toward the assailant. Keeping your strongest side forward enhances the speed, power, and accuracy of your first strike. This doesn't mean that you should never practice from your other side. You must be capable of de-escalating from both sides, and you should spend equal practice time on the left and right stances.

The de-escalation stance for grappling range.

Keep your hands open, relaxed and up to protect the upper gates of your centerline. Never drop your hands to your side, put your hands in your pocket, or cross your arms. You've got to have your hands up to strategically protect your anatomical targets and, if necessary, to fight back with your offensive techniques. Don't point your finger or clench your fists! Keep your hands loosely open, both facing the hostile person.

The hands are generally placed one behind the other in a staggered formation along your centerline. The lead arm is held high and bent at approximately 90 degrees. The rear arm is kept back. Arranged this way, the hands not only protect the torso centerline but also allow quick deployment of your body weapons. Finally, when holding your hand guard, do not tighten your shoulder or arm muscle. Stay relaxed and loose.

When assuming your de-escalation stance, place your feet about shoulder width apart. Keep your knees bent and flexible. Your weight distribution is also an important factor. Since self-defense is dynamic, your weight distribution will change frequently. However, when stationary, keep 50 percent of your body weight on each leg and always be in control of it.

De-escalation Stance Drill (Mirror Scenarios)

One of the best ways to develop and refine your de-escalation stance is to practice in front of a mirror. To begin, stand in front of a full-length mirror and picture a de-escalation scenario in your mind.

Envision a very angry and hostile person screaming at you. Once this scenario is crystal clear, assume the proper de-escalation stance and look into the mirror.

The 10 Best Bar Fighting Moves

Now, assess your stance while being cognizant of your physiology and hand positioning. Next, speak out loud and verbally defuse the situation with this imaginary hostile person. Remember to always use selective semantics (choice words) for your scenario.

Pictured here, two CFA students practice de-escalation scenarios.

To evaluate your performance, you may want to videotape the exercise. There are hundreds of possible de-escalation scenarios to practice. Here are a few to get you started:

- angry bar patron
- disgruntled employee
- angry spouse
- resentful relative
- irate customer or client
- drunken friend
- enraged motorist

- unbalanced street vagrant

- egotistical punk

- jealous or suspicious friend

- confrontation neighbor

- irate protester(s)

- quarrelsome religious fanatic

- argumentative street vendor

- mentally ill family member

6. Get Ready for Close-Quarter Fighting

Bar fighting is synonymous with close-quarter fighting. Unlike martial arts tournaments and cage fighting events, you will not be afforded the luxury of distance and space. In most cases, you're going to have to fight your adversary in a cramped space littered with both people and furniture.

Close-quarter combat will require the application of specific bar fighting technique. Some include the following:

ELBOWS

The elbows are devastating weapons that can be used in the grappling range. They are explosive, deceptive, and very difficult to stop. Elbows can generally be delivered horizontally, vertically, and diagonally. Targets include the assailant's temple, throat, chin, cervical vertebrae, ribs, and solar plexus. When delivering elbow strikes, be certain to pivot your hips and shoulder forcefully in the direction of your blow.

Vertical Elbow - The vertical elbow strike travels vertically to the assailant's face, throat, or body. It can be executed from either the right or left side of the body. To perform the strike, raise your elbow vertically (with the elbow flexed) until your hand is next to the side of your head. The striking surface is the point of the elbow. The power for this strike is acquired through the quick extension of the legs at the moment of impact.

Horizontal Elbow - The horizontal elbow strike travels horizontally to the assailant's face, throat, or body. It can also be executed from either the right or left side of the body. To perform the strike, begin from the on-guard hand position, then rotate your hips and shoulders horizontally into your target. Your palms should be facing downward with your hand next to the side of your head. The striking surface is the elbow point.

Diagonal Elbow (traveling downward) - The diagonal elbow strike travels diagonally downward to the assailant's face, throat, or body. It can be delivered from either the right or left side of the body. To execute the strike, rotate your elbow back, up, and over while quickly whipping it downward to your desired target. Bend your knees as your body descends with the strike. Your palm should be facing away from you when making contact. The striking surface is the elbow point.

KNEES

The knee strike is another devastating close- quarter grappling-range tool that can bring a formidable assailant to the ground instantly. The knee strike can be delivered vertically and diagonally to a variety of anatomical targets, including the common peroneal nerve, the quadriceps, the groin, the ribs, and, in some cases, the face. When delivering the knee strike, be certain to make contact with your patella and not your lower thigh. To guarantee sufficient power, deliver all your knee strikes with your rear leg.

USE YOUR HEAD

When engaged in close quarters, use your head for butting your assailant. Head butts are ideal when a strong attacker has placed you in a hold in which your arms are pinned against your sides. The head butt can be delivered in the following four directions:

(1) forward

(2) backward

(3) right side

(4) left side

FOOT STOMPING

The foot stomp is a deceptive close-quarter grappling technique that can cause excruciating pain for your assailant. To perform the foot stomp, raise your lead foot approximately 10 inches from the ground and forcibly stomp on the assailant's toes with the heel of your foot. If you doubt the effectiveness of a foot stomp, consider this sobering fact: a woman wearing high-heeled shoes can generate up to 1,600 pounds of pressure per square inch when delivering the foot stomp.

THUMB GOUGING

The double-thumb gouge is a nuclear grappling tactic that can produce devastating results. This tactic can be delivered when either standing or fighting on the ground. To perform the gouge, place one hand on each side of the assailant's face. Stabilize your hands by wrapping your fingers around both sides of your assailant's jaw. Immediately drive both your thumbs into the assailant's eye sockets. Maintain and increase forceful pressure. The double- thumb gouge can cause temporary or permanent blindness, shock, and unconsciousness. WARNING: The double-thumb gouge should only be used in life-and-death situations! Be certain that it is legally warranted and justified.

CRUSHING TECHNIQUES

Crushing techniques are another nuclear ground-fighting tactic that can be used either when standing or ground fighting with your adversary. The two primary crushing targets are your assailant's throat and testicles. When attacking the throat, make certain to drive your fingers deep into the assailant's trachea. Let them envelope the windpipe. Deliberately squeeze the pipe and try to crush it.

When crushing the testicles, grab deep into the assailant's groin region, attempting to isolate the testicles. Squeeze and crush them together as forcefully as you can.

WARNING: Crushing techniques should only be used in life-and-death situations! Make certain that your actions are legally and morally justified.

7. Hit Him First! Hit Him Fast! Hit Him Hard!

Whenever you are threatened by a dangerous adversary and there is no way to escape safely, you must strike first, strike fast, strike with authority, and keep the pressure on. This offensive strategy is known as my first-strike principle, and it's essential to the process of neutralizing a formidable adversary in a bar fight.

Basically, a first strike is defined as the strategic application of proactive force designed to interrupt the initial stages of an assault before it becomes a self-defense situation.

One inescapable fact about self-defense is that the longer the fight lasts, the greater your chances of serious injury or even death.

Chapter Two: The 10 Best Bar Fighting Moves

Common sense suggests that you must end the fight as quickly as possible. Striking first is the best method of achieving this tactical objective because it permits you to neutralize your barroom brawling assailant swiftly while, at the same time, precluding his ability to retaliate effectively. No time is wasted, and no unnecessary risks are taken.

When it comes to reality based self-defense, the element of surprise is invaluable. Launching the first strike gives you the upper hand because it allows you to hit the criminal adversary suddenly and unexpectedly. As a result, you demolish his defenses and ultimately take him out of the fight.

Employing the first-strike principle requires an offensive mentality that compels you to act rather than react. You must be aggressive and take affirmative and absolute control of the situation by making all the decisions and acting immediately without apprehension or trepidation.

Unfortunately, most martial art instructors teach their students to wait for their opponent to make the first move. Big mistake! In the dangerous and unforgiving rooms of many watering holes, this reactive type of approach will get you a one-way trip to the city morgue.

There are also self-defense practitioners who are simply too timid to take the initiative and hit first. Many won't strike first because they simply don't know how to execute a preemptive strike successfully. Others are uncertain about the legal requirements and justifications, and, as a result, they second-guess their instincts, hesitate, and end up kissing the beer soaked floors. Therefore, it's imperative that you have a basic understanding of the legal requirements of launching a preemptive strike in a self-defense situation.

So, When Can I Hit Him?

The most difficult aspect of the first-strike principle is determining exactly when a person can strike first. Well, because every bar fight is going to be different, there is no simple answer. However, there are some fundamental elements that must be present if you are going to launch a preemptive strike.

First, you must never use force against another person unless it is absolutely justified. Force is broken down into two levels: lethal and nonlethal. Lethal force is defined as the amount of force that can cause serious bodily injury or death. Nonlethal force is an amount of force that does not cause serious bodily injury or death.

Keep in mind that any time you use physical force against another person, you run the risk of having a civil suit filed against you. Anyone can hire a lawyer and file a suit for damages. Likewise, anyone can file a criminal complaint against you. Whether criminal charges will be brought against you depends upon the prosecutor's or grand jury's view of the facts. Nevertheless, I can tell you that if you are trained in the martial arts, you will be held to a much higher standard of behavior by a jury of your peers.

Second, the first-strike principle should only be used as an act of protection against unlawful injury or the immediate risk of unlawful injury. If you decide to launch a preemptive strike against your adversary, you'd better be certain that a reasonable threat exists and that it is absolutely necessary to protect yourself from immediate danger.

Please remember, the decision to launch a preemptive strike must always be a last resort, after all other means of avoiding violence have been exhausted.

First Strike Techniques

What follows are several effective first strike technique you can use in the tight confines of a bar.

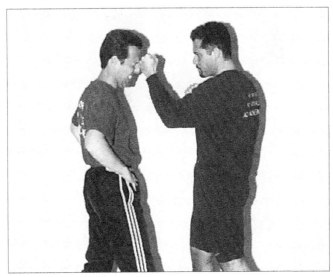

A short-arc hammer fist to the nose.

Finger jab to the eyes.

Palm heel to the chin.

Elbow strike to the face.

Push kick to the thigh.

The Head Butt.

If deadly force is warranted and justified, you can strike the assailant's throat with the web of your hand.

If distance permits, a vertical kick to the groin.

8. Improvised Weapons

A bar is loaded with makeshift weapons! Essentially, makeshift weapons (or MSW) are common, everyday objects that can be converted into either offensive or defensive hand-held weapons. However, for a MSW to be effective in a combat situation, it must be appropriate to the function you have assigned to it. For instance, you won't be able to knock someone out with a hot cup of coffee, but you could throw it into their eyes and temporarily blind them. Whereas you could knock someone unconscious with a good heavy flashlight but you could not use it to shield yourself from a knife attack. Makeshift weapons can be broken down into the following four types:

- Cutting
- Shielding
- Distracting
- Striking

Cutting makeshift weapons - these are objects or implements used to stab or slash your assailant. Examples include: darts, utility knives, forks, ice pick, screwdriver, broken glass, straight razor, pen, pencil, large nail, ice scraper, fire poker, crow bar, car keys, pitch fork, shovel, hack saw, knitting needle, spike, hatchet, meat hook, scissors, letter opener, cutting shears, trowel.

Shielding makeshift weapons - these are objects used to shield yourself from attack. Examples of shielding makeshift weapons include the following: barstools, briefcases, trash-can lids, bicycles, thick sofa cushions, backpacks, lawn chairs, drawers, cafeteria trays, suitcases, thick pillows, leather jackets/coats, sleeping bags, motorcycle helmets, small end tables, hubcaps, etc. Once again, be certain that your makeshift weapon has the structural integrity to get the job done effectively.

The 10 Best Bar Fighting Moves

Distracting makeshift weapons - these are objects that can be thrown into your assailant's face, torso, or legs to temporarily distract him. Generally distracting makeshift weapons are thrown into your assailant's face. Some examples include the following: billiard balls, barstools, sunglasses, magazines, car keys, wallets, ashtrays, books, salt shakers, alarm clocks, coins, bottles, bars of soap, shoes, dirt, sand, gravel, rocks, videotapes, small figurines, cassette tapes, watering can, hot liquids, paperweights, pesticide sprays, and oven cleaner spray.

Striking makeshift weapons - these are objects used to strike the assailant. Examples of striking makeshift weapons include billiard balls, barstools, beer mugs, sticks, bricks, crowbars, baseball bats, shovels, golf clubs, lamps, books, light chair, pool cues, pipes, heavy flashlights, hammers, binoculars, glass bottles, telephones, tool boxes, briefcases, car doors, canes, walking sticks, automobile, light dumbbells, 2 x 4s, etc.

Finally, there is some overlap between the various categories of make-shift weapons. For example, a large backpack can be thrown into an attacker's face for distraction or used to shield against a knife attack.

Something as simple as a roll of quarters can yield devastating results.

Tactical pens make great weapons improvised weapons.

Some tactical flashlights can be just as effective as a kubotan.

9. Strategic Positioning Before, During and After a Bar Fight

How and where you choose to position yourself will help minimize your risk and danger in the vent a fight breaks out. When I refer to "positioning" I'm talking about the spatial relationship between you and the assailant in terms of threat, tactical escape, target selection.

In combat, it's important to understand the strategic implications of the assailant's positioning prior to and during the fight. For example, is the assailant standing squarely in front of you or sideways? Is he mounted on top of you in a ground fight? Or is he inside your leg guard? What anatomical targets does the assailant present you with prior to lauding a preemptive strike? Is he blocking a door or any other escape route? Is his back to a light source? Is he close to your only possible makeshift weapon in the bar? Are multiple assailants closing in on you? Is your assailant firing his gun from a position of cover or concealment? You must answer these questions before choosing a tactical strategy appropriate to the situation.

What follows are a few tips for strategic positioning when first entering a bar:

- Whenever you enter a bar, try to sit close to an exit and always have an emergency escape route in mind in case you need to exit the place.

- When looking for a place to sit down, try to find a spot that allows you to keep your back to the wall. You never what to be surprise attacked from behind.

- When sitting at your table, get into the habit of constantly scanning the bar, thoroughly and quickly noting potential problems.

- If trouble is approaching you, get out of your seat and stand up immediately. Remember, it's very difficult to defend yourself when seated in chair or sitting on the barstool.

- If you have to use the restroom, always use a bathroom stall instead of a urinal.

- If the bar has mirrors or windows, get into the habit of frequently using these reflective sources to identify potential problems.

- Be especially careful when taking shortcuts to the bar. This includes alleys, parking lots, trails, tunnels, etc.

- Try to pick a seat or a table that has a light source behind you instead of in front of you.

- Park you car or vehicle in a spot that will allow you to quickly flee from the property. Avoid having you car blocked in by another vehicle.

- If a fight breaks out in the bar or any other drinking establishment, leave immediately. The entertainment value of watching a fight is not worth its potential danger.

10. Dress for the Occasion

What you wear can play a big role in the outcome of a bar fight. First, avoid wearing restrictive clothing that will limit arm or leg movement. For example, tight pants restrict knee strike techniques and the ability to run from danger, dress ties can be used to strangle, manipulate, or throw you off balance, and bulky winter coats can inhibit striking and grappling techniques. Also, light running shoes offer poor ankle support during lateral or otherwise evasive footwork. Earrings and nipple piercings can be torn from your body during a ground fight. Always try to wear clothes and shoes that facilitate quick and free movement. Leather jackets are good protection to the arms and extremities during a knife attack. Heavy athletic shoes (i.e., cross-trainers, court shoes) can enhance your footwork and kicking techniques.

Also, try to keep your hair short, especially at the back of your head. Long hair or ponytails can be dangerous and risky for the following reasons:

(1) Vision - they can temporarily impair your vision during the course of a compound attack or during a ground fight.

(2) Manipulation - in a grappling situation or ground fight your assailant can pull your hair and manipulate your balance as well as easily control you and throw you by the hair.

(3) Immobilization - your assailant can temporarily immobilize you by grabbing your hair.

Other Important Tips

- If you frequent a particular bar or night spot, always befriend the bouncers and know each of them by name.

- Since alcohol has a tendency to increase your assailant's pain threshold, you might have to strike your adversary harder and longer than usual.

- Try to keep your hands free and unoccupied as much as possible.

- Limit your conversation and avoid letting someone lure you into a conversation about a heated subject like religion, politics, and sports.

- Appear strong and always look calm, and confident when you enter a drinking establishment.

Chapter Two: The 10 Best Bar Fighting Moves

- Expect obstacles - people, barstools, pool tables, chairs, tables, etc., will get in your way when fighting

- Avoid calling attention to yourself with loud or boisterous behavior. You'll only be asking for trouble.

The 10 Best Bar Fighting Moves

Chapter Three
Training Tips and Suggestions

The 10 Best Bar Fighting Moves

The Best Ways to Prepare for a Bar Fight

In this chapter, I'm going to teach you specific drills and exercises that will prepare you for the possibility of a bar fight. Most of them are the culmination of years of research, analysis, and experimentation. I have used these exercises to teach thousands of students over the past three decades and I'm confident they will help you in your self-defense training. We will start with scenario-based training.

Scenario-Based Training

Scenario-based training uses scripts of real-world experiences to meet specific training objectives in a dangerous environment. This type of simulation training is ideal for developing the mental and physical skills you will need in a bar fight. What follows are two scenario-based drills that I regularly use with my students. They are de-escalation and tactical options training.

What is De-escalation?

As I stated earlier, De-escalation is the strategic process of diffusing a potentially violent confrontation. The goal is to eliminate the possibility of an agitated individual resorting to violence. De-escalation is a delicate mixture of science and art, psychology and warfare. It requires you to be in total control of yourself, both physically and emotionally in order to deal effectively with someone on the verge of losing control. Simply put, it is the art of "tactically calming" the aggressor.

As Real as it Gets!

Full-contact de-escalation training replicates the violence and danger of a real street confrontation. I have participated and instructed these mock scenarios for over thirty years, and I can tell you they are as real as it gets. The adrenaline dump created by de-escalation scenarios is almost identical to that of a real situation. In fact, most of my students have reported experiencing the very same anxiety, stress and fear of a real confrontation.

Full-contact de-escalation training requires a minimum of two people, however, advanced practitioners can participate in multiple attacker scenarios as well. When it comes to this type of exercise, safety is of paramount importance. Both you and your training partner must always wear protective gear (i.e. headgear, sparring gloves, mouthpiece, groin cup, etc).

This form of scenario-based training also requires both spontaneity and the element of the unknown. For example, during a typical scenario your partner will play the role of a very angry and hostile person. This requires him to act out using numerous signs of aggression, including yelling, swearing, threats, challenges, pacing back and forth, rapid forward movement, parental finger (pointing finger in chest or face), heavy breathing, clenched fists, taut neck, hunched shoulders, shoulder shifting, etc.

Next, you must attempt to diffuse his anger. This means using both verbal and nonverbal techniques to calm him down, while simultaneously employing physical safeguards. However, there's no guarantee that your de-escalation skills will work. There is always the possibility your training partner will attack no matter how skillful and sincere you are in your efforts to avoid violence. If your partner does decide to attack you, he must do so with 100% commitment.

There are an infinite number of de-escalation scenarios that you can practice. The following will get you started.

SCENARIO 1: You are in a crowded bar having a good time. As you turn around to move to the other side of the room, you accidentally spill your drink on a patron's shirt. He becomes angry and begins to yell at you for being so clumsy.

SCENARIO 2: You are hurriedly driving down the road, and you accidentally cut off another motorist. As you walk into the grocery store, you notice the presence of the same motorist. Angrily, he starts walking toward you.

SCENARIO 3: You are walking down a city street with your spouse when a vagrant suddenly approaches you, asking for money. You reply that you don't have anything to give him. He becomes angry and begins to yell obscenities at the both of you. De-escalate the situation.

SCENARIO 4: You are walking your date to her front door when suddenly you are confronted with her angry and jealous ex-boyfriend.

SCENARIO 5: You and your friend are watching a movie in a crowded theater. The two people in front of you continue to talk throughout the picture. You politely ask them to be quiet. The man turns around and tells you to shut up. You respond by telling him to keep his voice down. The man stands up and angrily invites you outside.

SCENARIO 6: You are at a party. One of your best friends is drunk and becomes a nuisance to everyone. He approaches you and mentions how he envies you. Within a few seconds, his admiration turns to jealousy and anger. He says that you are spoiled and disloyal. He pushes your shoulder in an attempt to provoke you to fight.

SCENARIO 7: Your close friend is extremely drunk and insists that he is capable of driving himself home. To prevent him from driving, you grab his car keys and put them in your pocket. He is angry and embarrassed that you have taken his keys and demands that you give them back.

The 10 Best Bar Fighting Moves

SCENARIO 8: You are driving through a residential neighborhood when suddenly a dog runs in front of your car. You immediately hit your brakes and get out to see what has happened. You notice that the dog is dead. A few seconds later, the owner of the dog arrives at the scene. She is hysterical and begins to scream at you for being so reckless.

SCENARIO 9: You have just pulled into a parking space at the shopping mall. As you open your car door, you accidentally slam it into the car parked next to you. The owner of the car gets out and begins to scream at you.

SCENARIO 10: You are at the beach, playing catch with your friend. As the ball is thrown to you, it accidentally lands in a sunbather's face. He jumps up and begins to threaten you.

Tactical Options Training

Tactical options training first requires you to rapidly gather and analyze information and then accurately evaluating it in terms of threat and danger. In general, you can assess people, places, actions, and objects.

What are the Tactical Options?

Accurate assessment skills will permit you to choose the appropriate tactical option. There are five tactical options to any self-defense situation. They are listed here in order of increasing level of resistance.

Comply - means to obey the assailant's commands. For example, if you are held at gunpoint (out of disarming range) for the purpose of robbery, there is nothing to do but comply. Take out your wallet, take off your watch, hand over your car keys, do what you are told. Comply

Escape - or tactical retreat means to flee from the threat or danger safely and rapidly. For example, if you are being held hostage and your captor is distracted long enough for you to escape safely, then do it.

De-escalate - means the art and science of diffusing a hostile individual. Not every confrontation warrants fighting back. Often you will be able to use de-escalation skills to talk someone out of a possible violent encounter.

Assert -means standing up for you and your rights. Through effective communication skills, you can thwart a person's efforts to intimidate, dominate, and control you.

Fight back - means using various physical and psychological tactics and techniques to stun, incapacitate, cripple or kill your attacker(s). For example, you're trapped in a dead-end alley by a knife-wielding psychotic who appears determined to butcher you. Your only option is to fight back!

These are just a few of the many possible examples of the five tactical responses. Every self-defense situation is different, and, moreover, most situations can be fluid. A dangerous situation might present an escape option at one moment but quickly turn into a fight-back situation at the next. For example, let's say you are kidnapped, and your captor leaves a door unlocked, and in your effort to escape, you run into him on your way out. Obviously, that is the time to fight for your life.

How Does it Work?

Tactical options training replicates the stress and anxiety of a real crisis situation. This exercise requires a minimum of two people donned in protective gear (i.e. headgear, sparring gloves, mouthpiece, groin cup, etc.).

The 10 Best Bar Fighting Moves

Tactical options training is similar to de-escalation scenarios. However, it differs because you have five options (comply, escape, de-escalate, assert, and fight back) to choose from, instead of just one.

This scenario-based training also requires both spontaneity and the element of the unknown. During a training scenario, your partner plays the role of any person and character he wishes. For example, he can be a concerned citizen, nosy next-door neighbor, an annoying coworker, intoxicated vagrant, arrogant classmate, enraged friend, etc.

Next, your training partner approaches you and initiate a conversation that is relevant to his character. For example, if he's playing the role of the drunk, he might stumble about and ask you for money.

During the course of conversation, you must use your perception skills to assess the possible source of danger. In this case, what is this person's purpose in confronting you? Does he intend to rob you? Is he seeking retribution for something you may have done? Or is he simply looking to make some simple conversation with you? What is he saying and doing? How close is he? Where are his hands?

Pay very close attention to all available clues, especially nonverbal indicators. Your answers to these important questions will shape your overall tactical response. Let all of your five senses go to work to extract the necessary information. And don't forget to listen to what your instincts are telling you about this person.

Once you assess the situation promptly and accurately, you must reach a rational conclusion and choose the appropriate tactical response (i.e., comply, escape, de-escalate, assert or fight back). For instance, if your partner is acting like an irate motorist, your tactical option might be de-escalation skills. Likewise, if he plays the role of an unarmed street attacker, you'll have to fight back to ensure your survival.

A word of caution! You must always be alert when participating in this exercise. Don't become complacent and comfortable. Never assume there is no danger! Remember, there is always the possibility your training partner will attack you!

Full-Contact Sparring

Full-contact sparring is a practical method for developing instrumental aggression, attention control, self-confidence, immediate resilience, and arousal control. It also develops many physical attributes like speed, quickness, coordination, agility, timing, distancing, ambidexterity, endurance, flexibility, tactile sensitivity, pain tolerance, finesse, accuracy, and non-telegraphic movement.

Sparring skills require combining kicks and punches into fluid and logical combinations. Basic sparring sessions are conducted at a moderate and controlled pace. The good news is you can spar just about anywhere, such as a gym, basement, garage and even outdoors. However, before you begin training, you'll need protective head gear, 14 oz boxing gloves, and a mouth piece.

Depending on your level of conditioning, sparring rounds can range anywhere from one to five minutes. Each round is separated by either 30-second, one-minute or two-minute breaks. A good sparring session consists of at least five to eight rounds.

Since sparring workouts are structured around time, you will need a good workout timer. Most workout timers will allow you to adjust your round lengths anywhere from 30 seconds to 9 minutes. Rest periods can be changed from 30 seconds to 5 minutes depending on your level of conditioning and training goals.

When You Get Hit!

If and when you get hit in a sparring session, stay in control of your emotions and don't panic. Keep both hands up, stay mobile, and remain defensively alert. Maintain proper breathing, employ positive self-talk, and don't allow negative thoughts to contaminate your mind. Stay focused on the task at hand and continue to look for openings in your training partner's defenses.

Here are ten common mistakes that are made when sparring. Overcoming these errors will significantly enhance your fighting ability.

- Quitting or giving up after being hit.
- Being distracted (internally or externally) when fighting.
- Fearful or excessive blinking.
- Randomly throwing punches or failing to focus on a particular target.
- Lack of commitment when attacking your partner.
- Hesitating or over thinking.
- Turning your head away or closing your eyes when a blow is thrown at you.
- Turning your body completely sideways from the sparring partner.
- Running away from your opponent's attack.
- Nervously swatting your sparring partner's boxing glove.

Circle Combat Drill

This drill is conducted by having approximately 5 participants form a large circle (approximately 12 feet in diameter) around one person standing in the center. All of the participants must wear protective gear.

The drill begins with the instructor randomly selecting participants from the circle to attack the person in the middle. The defender must immediately identify and react to the attack using various defensive skills and techniques. Once the attacker finishes his assault, he returns to the circle, and the instructor immediately calls out another attacker. Once the practitioners become familiar with this drill, the instructor can make it more difficult by speeding up the selection of attackers, calling out multiple attackers at once, incorporating bludgeon and knife attacks, and even having the attackers take the fight to the ground.

Circle combat can last anywhere from 30 seconds to 5 minutes. It's up to the coach and the student's level of conditioning.

The Three Training Methodologies

There are also three specific training methodologies used to develop the fundamental skills of armed and unarmed fighting. They are proficiency training, conditioning training, and street training. Let's take a look at each one.

Proficiency Training

Proficiency training develops important attributes like self-discipline, immediate resilience, and attention control. When conducted properly, it also develops speed, power, accuracy, non-telegraphic movement, balance, and psychomotor skills. The training objective is to sharpen one specific body weapon, maneuver, or technique at a time by executing it over and over for a prescribed number of repetitions. Each time the technique is executed with clean form at various speeds. Movements can also be performed with your eyes closed to develop a kinesthetic feel for the action.

Proficiency training can be accomplished through the use of various types of equipment, including the heavy bag, double-end bag, focus mitts, training knives, mock pistols, striking shields, shin and knee guards, foam and plastic bats, mannequin heads, and so on.

Conditioning Training

The next methodology is conditioning training, and it's used for developing self-confidence and immediate resilience. Conditioning training also develops endurance, fluidity, rhythm, distancing, timing, speed, footwork, and balance.

Conditioning training can be performed on various pieces of equipment, including the heavy bag, double-end bag, focus mitts, body opponent bag, and against imaginary assailants in shadow fighting.

In most cases, conditioning training requires the practitioner to deliver a variety of fighting combinations for three or four-minute rounds separated by 30-second breaks. Like proficiency training, this type of training can also be performed at various speeds. A good workout consists of at least five rounds. Conditioning training is not necessarily limited to just three or four-minute rounds. For example, in some of my classes, I will have advanced students ground fighting for 30 minutes or longer.

Street Training

Street training is primarily used for developing instrumental aggression. However, it also improves speed, power, explosiveness, target selection and recognition, timing, footwork, pacing, and breath control.

Street training prepares you for the sudden stress and immediate fatigue of a real fight. Since many violent altercations are explosive, lasting an average of twenty seconds, you must train for this possible scenario. This means delivering explosive and powerful compound attacks with vicious intent for approximately twenty seconds, resting one minute, and then repeating the process.

You should practice this training methodology in different lighting, on different terrains, and in different environmental settings. You can use different types of training equipment as well. For example, you can prepare yourself for multiple assailants by having your training partners attack you with focus mitts from a variety of angles, ranges, and target postures. For twenty seconds, go after them with vicious low-line kicks, powerful punches, and devastating strikes.

Reality Based Self-Defense Training

As I mentioned in an earlier chapter, combat drills are the ideal vehicle for preparing you for a fight. In fact, you might want to take your training one step further by seeking hands-on training from a qualified reality based self-defense (RBSD) instructor.

Finding a Good School

However, you must be very cautious when choosing a martial art or self-defense school; they don't all have the same objectives. Here are some important points to consider before selecting a reality based self-defense (RBSD) school for self-defense training.

First, don't select a school because of its geographical proximity. You must always choose the school that best suits your needs. Don't let your laziness force you to sacrifice quality combat instruction. Also, don't choose a school because of its aesthetics. Just because a particular studio has a juice bar or fancy equipment doesn't guarantee quality instruction. Ironically, some of the best self-defense instruction can be provided in garages, basements, school gymnasiums, public parks, and college campuses.

The 10 Best Bar Fighting Moves

Obviously, finding a good school won't be easy, so plan to devote some time to the task. You might try looking in the Yellow Pages, on-line, or asking a friend if he or she knows of any reputable places. Or you may consider calling your local police department for some suggestions. Universities and community colleges can sometimes be good places to look for quality self-defense instruction. With patience, research, and some common sense, you'll find a good one.

When you do visit a school, be certain to watch a few of the classes. Evaluate what you see before making a choice. Consider the following questions: Is the environment conducive to real world combat training? Does the instructor offer stress inoculation training? What types of arousal control techniques does he teach? Is the class physically demanding? Are the combat drills practical and realistic? Are the skills and techniques uncomplicated? What type of training equipment do they use? After the class is over, ask a few students if they are satisfied with the classes.

Make certain the school is strictly devoted to the art and science of real world combat. It should also be eclectic, drawing from such fields as martial arts, criminal justice, military and police science, psychology, sociology, conflict management, histrionics, physics, kinesics, anatomy, physiology, kinesiology, and emergency medicine. Other factors to consider before selecting a RBSD school include:

- What is the cost? Can you live with the financial terms?
- Are private or semiprivate lessons offered?
- Are questions permitted during class?
- What components of mental toughness are taught in class?
- Does the school stress range proficiency?
- Does the school emphasize the legal ramifications of self-defense?

- Are full-contact drills a regular part of the training curriculum?

- Are children and adults taught together in the same class?

- Is weapon instruction (firearms, knives, impact tools, OC sprays, etc.) offered?

- Are training materials (i.e., books, manuals, videos, etc.) available to the students?

- How many times per week can you attend class?

Finding a Good Instructor

You must also consider the instructor's qualifications and experience. In fact, you should choose a self-defense instructor the very same way that you would choose a surgeon to perform a difficult operation.

Since there is no standardized requirement for teaching RBSD, you're going to have to find out as much as you can about the instructor. Don't hesitate to ask a few questions about his background and credentials. If he's legitimate, he will understand your concern. Here are the questions to get answers to when selecting a competent instructor:

- How long has the instructor been studying RBSD?

- How long has the instructor been teaching RBSD?

- Exactly which aspects of self-defense is the instructor qualified to teach?

- What agency, institution, or individual certified the instructor?

- Is the instructor well known (locally or nationally) for his or her expertise?

- Is the instructor articulate and knowledgeable about criminal violence?

- Does the instructor practice what he or she preaches?

- Does the instructor look the part? Is he or she in shape?

- Does the instructor teach the military or law enforcement agencies?

- Does the instructor teach self-defense for a living? Or is it a part-time job?

- Does the instructor project a professional image?

- Does the instructor answer all of your questions?

- Does the instructor's attitude show patience and respect toward his students?

- Does the instructor seem genuinely concerned about your needs, or is he shoving a contract in your face?

Enrolling in a good RBSD school is a worthwhile investment. Along with learning life-saving combat skills, you'll also acquire a variety of other personal attributes such as physical fitness, personal empowerment, and self-discipline. Mind-body-spirit unification, self-confidence, and emotional control are also common residuals of serious instruction. But most importantly, with good self-defense training you will acquire a renewed appreciation of personal protection.

The 10 Best Bar Fighting Moves

Glossary

The following terms are defined in the context of Contemporary Fighting Arts and its related concepts. In many instances, the definitions bear little resemblance to those found in a standard dictionary.

A

accuracy—The precise or exact projection of force. Accuracy is also defined as the ability to execute a combative movement with precision and exactness.

adaptability—The ability to physically and psychologically adjust to new or different conditions or circumstances of combat.

advanced first-strike tools—Offensive techniques that are specifically used when confronted with multiple opponents.

aerobic exercise—Literally, "with air." Exercise that elevates the heart rate to a training level for a prolonged period of time, usually 30 minutes.

affective preparedness – One of the three components of preparedness. Affective preparedness means being emotionally, philosophically, and spiritually prepared for the strains of combat. See cognitive preparedness and psychomotor preparedness.

aggression—Hostile and injurious behavior directed toward a person.

aggressive response—One of the three possible counters when assaulted by a grab, choke, or hold from a standing position. Aggressive response requires you to counter the enemy with destructive blows and strikes. See moderate response and passive response.

aggressive hand positioning—Placement of hands so as to imply aggressive or hostile intentions.

agility—An attribute of combat. One's ability to move his or her body quickly and gracefully.

amalgamation—A scientific process of uniting or merging.

ambidextrous—The ability to perform with equal facility on both the right and left sides of the body.

anabolic steroids – synthetic chemical compounds that resemble the male sex hormone testosterone. This performance-enhancing drug is known to increase lean muscle mass, strength, and endurance.

analysis and integration—One of the five elements of CFA's mental component. This is the painstaking process of breaking down various elements, concepts, sciences, and disciplines into their atomic parts, and then methodically and strategically analyzing, experimenting, and drastically modifying the information so that it fulfills three combative requirements: efficiency, effectiveness, and safety. Only then is it finally integrated into the CFA system.

anatomical striking targets—The various anatomical body targets that can be struck and which are especially vulnerable to potential harm. They include: the eyes, temple, nose, chin, back of neck, front of neck, solar plexus, ribs, groin, thighs, knees, shins, and instep.

anchoring – The strategic process of trapping the assailant's neck or limb in order to control the range of engagement during razing.

assailant—A person who threatens or attacks another person.

assault—The threat or willful attempt to inflict injury upon the person of another.

assault and battery—The unlawful touching of another person without justification.

assessment—The process of rapidly gathering, analyzing, and accurately evaluating information in terms of threat and danger. You can assess people, places, actions, and objects.

attack—Offensive action designed to physically control, injure, or kill another person.

attack by combination (ABC) - One of the five methods of attack. See compound attack.

attack by drawing (ABD) - One of the five methods of attack. A method of attack predicated on counterattack.

attitude—One of the three factors that determine who wins a street fight. Attitude means being emotionally, philosophically, and spiritually liberated from societal and religious mores. See skills and knowledge.

attributes of combat—The physical, mental, and spiritual qualities that enhance combat skills and tactics.

awareness—Perception or knowledge of people, places, actions, and objects. (In CFA, there are three categories of tactical awareness: criminal awareness, situational awareness, and self-awareness.)

B

balance—One's ability to maintain equilibrium while stationary or moving.

blading the body—Strategically positioning your body at a 45-degree angle.

blitz and disengage—A style of sparring whereby a fighter moves into a range of combat, unleashes a strategic compound attack, and then quickly disengages to a safe distance. Of all sparring methodologies, the blitz and disengage most closely resembles a real street fight.

block—A defensive tool designed to intercept the assailant's attack by placing a non-vital target between the assailant's strike and your vital body target.

body composition—The ratio of fat to lean body tissue.

body language—Nonverbal communication through posture, gestures, and facial expressions.

body mechanics—Technically precise body movement during the execution of a body weapon, defensive technique, or other fighting maneuver.

body tackle – A tackle that occurs when your opponent haphazardly rushes forward and plows his body into yours.

body weapon—Also known as a tool, one of the various body parts that can be used to strike or otherwise injure or kill a criminal assailant.

burn out—A negative emotional state acquired by physically over- training. Some symptoms include: illness, boredom, anxiety, disinterest in training, and general sluggishness.

C

cadence—Coordinating tempo and rhythm to establish a timing pattern of movement.

cardiorespiratory conditioning—The component of physical fitness that deals with the heart, lungs, and circulatory system.

centerline—An imaginary vertical line that divides your body in half and which contains many of your vital anatomical targets.

choke holds—Holds that impair the flow of blood or oxygen to the brain.

circular movements—Movements that follow the direction of a curve.

close-quarter combat—One of the three ranges of knife and

bludgeon combat. At this distance, you can strike, slash, or stab your assailant with a variety of close-quarter techniques.

cognitive development—One of the five elements of CFA's mental component. The process of developing and enhancing your fighting skills through specific mental exercises and techniques. See analysis and integration, killer instinct, philosophy, and strategic/tactical development.

cognitive exercises—Various mental exercises used to enhance fighting skills and tactics.

cognitive preparedness – One of the three components of preparedness. Cognitive preparedness means being equipped with the strategic concepts, principles, and general knowledge of combat. See affective preparedness and psychomotor preparedness.

combat-oriented training—Training that is specifically related to the harsh realities of both armed and unarmed combat. See ritual-oriented training and sport-oriented training.

combative arts—The various arts of war. See martial arts.

combative attributes—See attributes of combat.

combative fitness—A state characterized by cardiorespiratory and muscular/skeletal conditioning, as well as proper body composition.

combative mentality—Also known as the killer instinct, this is a combative state of mind necessary for fighting. See killer instinct.

combat ranges—The various ranges of unarmed combat.

combative utility—The quality of condition of being combatively useful.

combination(s)—See compound attack.

common peroneal nerve—A pressure point area located approximately four to six inches above the knee on the midline of the outside of the thigh.

composure—A combative attribute. Composure is a quiet and focused mind-set that enables you to acquire your combative agenda.

compound attack—One of the five conventional methods of attack. Two or more body weapons launched in strategic succession whereby the fighter overwhelms his assailant with a flurry of full speed, full-force blows.

conditioning training—A CFA training methodology requiring the practitioner to deliver a variety of offensive and defensive combinations for a 4-minute period. See proficiency training and street training.

contact evasion—Physically moving or manipulating your body to avoid being tackled by the adversary.

Contemporary Fighting Arts—A modern martial art and self-defense system made up of three parts: physical, mental, and spiritual.

conventional ground-fighting tools—Specific ground-fighting techniques designed to control, restrain, and temporarily incapacitate your adversary. Some conventional ground fighting tactics include: submission holds, locks, certain choking techniques, and specific striking techniques.

coordination—A physical attribute characterized by the ability to perform a technique or movement with efficiency, balance, and accuracy.

counterattack—Offensive action made to counter an assailant's initial attack.

courage—A combative attribute. The state of mind and spirit that enables a fighter to face danger and vicissitudes with confidence, resolution, and bravery.

creatine monohydrate—A tasteless and odorless white powder that mimics some of the effects of anabolic steroids. Creatine is a safe body-building product that can benefit anyone who wants to increase their strength, endurance, and lean muscle mass.

criminal awareness—One of the three categories of CFA awareness. It involves a general understanding and knowledge of the nature and dynamics of a criminal's motivations, mentalities, methods, and capabilities to perpetrate violent crime. See situational awareness and self-awareness.

criminal justice—The study of criminal law and the procedures associated with its enforcement.

criminology—The scientific study of crime and criminals.

cross-stepping—The process of crossing one foot in front of or behind the other when moving.

crushing tactics—Nuclear grappling-range techniques designed to crush the assailant's anatomical targets.

D

deadly force—Weapons or techniques that may result in unconsciousness, permanent disfigurement, or death.

deception—A combative attribute. A stratagem whereby you delude your assailant.

decisiveness—A combative attribute. The ability to follow a tactical course of action that is unwavering and focused.

defense—The ability to strategically thwart an assailant's attack (armed or unarmed).

defensive flow—A progression of continuous defensive responses.

defensive mentality—A defensive mind-set.

defensive reaction time—The elapsed time between an assailant's physical attack and your defensive response to that attack. See offensive reaction time.

demeanor—A person's outward behavior. One of the essential factors to consider when assessing a threatening individual.

diet—A lifestyle of healthy eating.

disingenuous vocalization—The strategic and deceptive utilization of words to successfully launch a preemptive strike at your adversary.

distancing—The ability to quickly understand spatial relationships and how they relate to combat.

distractionary tactics—Various verbal and physical tactics designed to distract your adversary.

double-end bag—A small leather ball hung from the ceiling and anchored to the floor with bungee cord. It helps develop striking accuracy, speed, timing, eye-hand coordination, footwork and overall defensive skills.

double-leg takedown—A takedown that occurs when your opponent shoots for both of your legs to force you to the ground.

E

ectomorph—One of the three somatotypes. A body type characterized by a high degree of slenderness, angularity, and fragility. See endomorph and mesomorph.

effectiveness—One of the three criteria for a CFA body weapon, technique, tactic, or maneuver. It means the ability to produce a desired effect. See efficiency and safety.

efficiency—One of the three criteria for a CFA body weapon, technique, tactic, or maneuver. It means the ability to reach an objective quickly and economically. See effectiveness and safety.

emotionless—A combative attribute. Being temporarily devoid of human feeling.

endomorph—One of the three somatotypes. A body type characterized by a high degree of roundness, softness, and body fat. See ectomorph and mesomorph.

evasion—A defensive maneuver that allows you to strategically maneuver your body away from the assailant's strike.

evasive sidestepping—Evasive footwork where the practitioner moves to either the right or left side.

evasiveness—A combative attribute. The ability to avoid threat or danger.

excessive force—An amount of force that exceeds the need for a particular event and is unjustified in the eyes of the law.

experimentation—The painstaking process of testing a combative hypothesis or theory.

explosiveness—A combative attribute that is characterized by a sudden outburst of violent energy.

F

fear—A strong and unpleasant emotion caused by the anticipation or awareness of threat or danger. There are three stages of fear in order of intensity: fright, panic, and terror. See fright, panic, and terror.

feeder—A skilled technician who manipulates the focus mitts.

femoral nerve—A pressure point area located approximately 6 inches above the knee on the inside of the thigh.

fighting stance—Any one of the stances used in CFA's system. A strategic posture you can assume when face-to-face with an unarmed assailant(s). The fighting stance is generally used after you have launched your first-strike tool.

fight-or-flight syndrome—A response of the sympathetic nervous system to a fearful and threatening situation, during which it prepares your body to either fight or flee from the perceived danger.

finesse—A combative attribute. The ability to skillfully execute a movement or a series of movements with grace and refinement.

first strike—Proactive force used to interrupt the initial stages of an assault before it becomes a self-defense situation.

first-strike principle—A CFA principle that states that when physical danger is imminent and you have no other tactical option but to fight back, you should strike first, strike fast, and strike with authority and keep the pressure on.

first-strike stance—One of the stances used in CFA's system. A strategic posture used prior to initiating a first strike.

first-strike tools—Specific offensive tools designed to initiate a preemptive strike against your adversary.

fisted blows – Hand blows delivered with a clenched fist.

five tactical options – The five strategic responses you can make in a self-defense situation, listed in order of increasing level of resistance: comply, escape, de-escalate, assert, and fight back.

flexibility—The muscles' ability to move through maximum natural ranges. See muscular/skeletal conditioning.

focus mitts—Durable leather hand mitts used to develop and sharpen offensive and defensive skills.

footwork—Quick, economical steps performed on the balls of the feet while you are relaxed, alert, and balanced. Footwork is structured around four general movements: forward, backward, right, and left.

fractal tool—Offensive or defensive tools that can be used in more than one combat range.

fright—The first stage of fear; quick and sudden fear. See panic and terror.

full Beat – One of the four beat classifications in the Widow Maker Program. The full beat strike has a complete initiation and retraction phase.

G

going postal - a slang term referring to a person who suddenly and unexpectedly attacks you with an explosive and frenzied flurry of blows. Also known as postal attack.

grappling range—One of the three ranges of unarmed combat. Grappling range is the closest distance of unarmed combat from which you can employ a wide variety of close-quarter tools and techniques. The grappling range of unarmed combat is also divided into two planes: vertical (standing) and horizontal (ground fighting). See kicking range and punching range.

grappling-range tools—The various body tools and techniques that are employed in the grappling range of unarmed combat, including head butts; biting, tearing, clawing, crushing, and gouging tactics; foot stomps, horizontal, vertical, and diagonal elbow strikes, vertical and diagonal knee strikes, chokes, strangles, joint locks, and holds. See punching range tools and kicking range tools.

ground fighting—Also known as the horizontal grappling plane, this is fighting that takes place on the ground.

guard—Also known as the hand guard, this refers to a fighter's hand positioning.

guard position—Also known as leg guard or scissors hold, this is a ground-fighting position in which a fighter is on his back holding his opponent between his legs.

H

half beat – One of the four beat classifications in the Widow Maker Program. The half beat strike is delivered through the retraction phase of the proceeding strike.

hand immobilization attack (HIA) - One of the five methods of attack. A method of attack whereby the practitioner traps his opponent's limb or limbs in order to execute an offense attack of his own.

hand positioning—See guard.

hand wraps—Long strips of cotton that are wrapped around the hands and wrists for greater protection.

haymaker—A wild and telegraphed swing of the arms executed by an unskilled fighter.

head-hunter—A fighter who primarily attacks the head.

heavy bag—A large cylindrical bag used to develop kicking, punching, or striking power.

high-line kick—One of the two different classifications of a kick. A kick that is directed to targets above an assailant's waist level. See low-line kick.

hip fusing—A full-contact drill that teaches a fighter to "stand his ground" and overcome the fear of exchanging blows with a stronger opponent. This exercise is performed by connecting two fighters with a 3-foot chain, forcing them to fight in the punching range of unarmed combat.

histrionics—The field of theatrics or acting.

hook kick—A circular kick that can be delivered in both kicking and punching ranges.

hook punch—A circular punch that can be delivered in both the punching and grappling ranges.

I

impact power—Destructive force generated by mass and velocity.

impact training—A training exercise that develops pain tolerance.

incapacitate—To disable an assailant by rendering him unconscious or damaging his bones, joints, or organs.

initiative—Making the first offensive move in combat.

inside position—The area between the opponent's arms, where he has the greatest amount of control.

intent—One of the essential factors to consider when assessing a threatening individual. The assailant's purpose or motive. See demeanor, positioning, range, and weapon capability.

intuition—The innate ability to know or sense something without the use of rational thought.

J

jeet kune do (JKD) - "Way of the intercepting fist." Bruce Lee's approach to the martial arts, which includes his innovative concepts, theories, methodologies, and philosophies.

jersey Pull – Strategically pulling the assailant's shirt or jacket over his head as he disengages from the clinch position.

joint lock—A grappling-range technique that immobilizes the assailant's joint.

K

The 10 Best Bar Fighting Moves

kick—A sudden, forceful strike with the foot.

kicking range—One of the three ranges of unarmed combat. Kicking range is the furthest distance of unarmed combat wherein you use your legs to strike an assailant. See grappling range and punching range.

kicking-range tools—The various body weapons employed in the kicking range of unarmed combat, including side kicks, push kicks, hook kicks, and vertical kicks.

killer instinct—A cold, primal mentality that surges to your consciousness and turns you into a vicious fighter.

kinesics—The study of nonlinguistic body movement communications. (For example, eye movement, shrugs, or facial gestures.)

kinesiology—The study of principles and mechanics of human movement.

kinesthetic perception—The ability to accurately feel your body during the execution of a particular movement.

knowledge—One of the three factors that determine who will win a street fight. Knowledge means knowing and understanding how to fight. See skills and attitude.

L

lead side -The side of the body that faces an assailant.

leg guard—See guard position.

linear movement—Movements that follow the path of a straight line.

low-maintenance tool—Offensive and defensive tools that require the least amount of training and practice to maintain proficiency. Low

140

maintenance tools generally do not require preliminary stretching.

low-line kick—One of the two different classifications of a kick. A kick that is directed to targets below the assailant's waist level. (See high-line kick.)

lock—See joint lock.

M

maneuver—To manipulate into a strategically desired position.

MAP—An acronym that stands for moderate, aggressive, passive. MAP provides the practitioner with three possible responses to various grabs, chokes, and holds that occur from a standing position. See aggressive response, moderate response, and passive response.

martial arts—The "arts of war."

masking—The process of concealing your true feelings from your opponent by manipulating and managing your body language.

mechanics—(See body mechanics.)

mental attributes—The various cognitive qualities that enhance your fighting skills.

mental component—One of the three vital components of the CFA system. The mental component includes the cerebral aspects of fighting including the killer instinct, strategic and tactical development, analysis and integration, philosophy, and cognitive development. See physical component and spiritual component.

mesomorph—One of the three somatotypes. A body type classified by a high degree of muscularity and strength. The mesomorph possesses the ideal physique for unarmed combat. See ectomorph and endomorph.

mobility—A combative attribute. The ability to move your body quickly and freely while balanced. See footwork.

moderate response—One of the three possible counters when assaulted by a grab, choke, or hold from a standing position. Moderate response requires you to counter your opponent with a control and restraint (submission hold). See aggressive response and passive response.

modern martial art—A pragmatic combat art that has evolved to meet the demands and characteristics of the present time.

mounted position—A dominant ground-fighting position where a fighter straddles his opponent.

muscular endurance—The muscles' ability to perform the same motion or task repeatedly for a prolonged period of time.

muscular flexibility—The muscles' ability to move through maximum natural ranges.

muscular strength—The maximum force that can be exerted by a particular muscle or muscle group against resistance.

muscular/skeletal conditioning—An element of physical fitness that entails muscular strength, endurance, and flexibility.

N

naked choke—A throat choke executed from the chest to back position. This secure choke is executed with two hands and it can be performed while standing, kneeling, and ground fighting with the opponent.

neck crush – A powerful pain compliance technique used when the adversary buries his head in your chest to avoid being razed.

neutralize—See incapacitate.

neutral zone—The distance outside the kicking range at which neither the practitioner nor the assailant can touch the other.

nonaggressive physiology—Strategic body language used prior to initiating a first strike.

nontelegraphic movement—Body mechanics or movements that do not inform an assailant of your intentions.

nuclear ground-fighting tools—Specific grappling range tools designed to inflict immediate and irreversible damage. Nuclear tools and tactics include biting tactics, tearing tactics, crushing tactics, continuous choking tactics, gouging techniques, raking tactics, and all striking techniques.

O

offense—The armed and unarmed means and methods of attacking a criminal assailant.

offensive flow—Continuous offensive movements (kicks, blows, and strikes) with unbroken continuity that ultimately neutralize or terminate the opponent. See compound attack.

offensive reaction time—The elapsed time between target selection and target impaction.

one-mindedness—A state of deep concentration wherein you are free from all distractions (internal and external).

ostrich defense—One of the biggest mistakes one can make when defending against an opponent. This is when the practitioner looks away from that which he fears (punches, kicks, and strikes). His mentality is, "If I can't see it, it can't hurt me."

P

pain tolerance—Your ability to physically and psychologically withstand pain.

panic—The second stage of fear; overpowering fear. See fright and terror.

parry—A defensive technique: a quick, forceful slap that redirects an assailant's linear attack. There are two types of parries: horizontal and vertical.

passive response—One of the three possible counters when assaulted by a grab, choke, or hold from a standing position. Passive response requires you to nullify the assault without injuring your adversary. See aggressive response and moderate response.

patience—A combative attribute. The ability to endure and tolerate difficulty.

perception—Interpretation of vital information acquired from your senses when faced with a potentially threatening situation.

philosophical resolution—The act of analyzing and answering various questions concerning the use of violence in defense of yourself and others.

philosophy—One of the five aspects of CFA's mental component. A deep state of introspection whereby you methodically resolve critical questions concerning the use of force in defense of yourself or others.

physical attributes—The numerous physical qualities that enhance your combative skills and abilities.

physical component—One of the three vital components of the CFA system. The physical component includes the physical aspects of fighting, such as physical fitness, weapon/technique mastery, and combative attributes. See mental component and spiritual component.

physical conditioning—See combative fitness.

physical fitness—See combative fitness.

positional asphyxia—The arrangement, placement, or positioning of your opponent's body in such a way as to interrupt your breathing and cause unconsciousness or possibly death.

positioning—The spatial relationship of the assailant to the assailed person in terms of target exposure, escape, angle of attack, and various other strategic considerations.

postal attack - see going postal.

power—A physical attribute of armed and unarmed combat. The amount of force you can generate when striking an anatomical target.

power generators—Specific points on your body that generate impact power. There are three anatomical power generators: shoulders, hips, and feet.

precision—See accuracy.

preemptive strike—See first strike.

premise—An axiom, concept, rule, or any other valid reason to modify or go beyond that which has been established.

preparedness—A state of being ready for combat. There are three components of preparedness: affective preparedness, cognitive preparedness, and psychomotor preparedness.

probable reaction dynamics - The opponent's anticipated or predicted movements or actions during both armed and unarmed combat.

proficiency training—A CFA training methodology requiring the practitioner to execute a specific body weapon, technique, maneuver, or tactic over and over for a prescribed number of repetitions. See conditioning training and street training.

progressive indirect attack (PIA) – One of the five methods of attack. A progressive method of attack whereby the initial tool or technique is designed to set the opponent up for follow-up blows.

proxemics—The study of the nature and effect of man's personal space.

proximity—The ability to maintain a strategically safe distance from a threatening individual.

pseudospeciation—A combative attribute. The tendency to assign subhuman and inferior qualities to a threatening assailant.

psychological conditioning—The process of conditioning the mind for the horrors and rigors of real combat.

psychomotor preparedness—One of the three components of preparedness. Psychomotor preparedness means possessing all of the physical skills and attributes necessary to defeat a formidable adversary. See affective preparedness and cognitive preparedness.

punch—A quick, forceful strike of the fists.

punching range—One of the three ranges of unarmed combat. Punching range is the mid range of unarmed combat from which the fighter uses his hands to strike his assailant. See kicking range and grappling range.

punching-range tools—The various body weapons that are employed in the punching range of unarmed combat, including finger jabs, palm-heel strikes, rear cross, knife-hand strikes, horizontal and shovel hooks, uppercuts, and hammer-fist strikes. See grappling-range tools and kicking-range tools.

Q

qualities of combat—See attributes of combat.

quarter beat - One of the four beat classifications of the Widow Maker Program. Quarter beat strikes never break contact with the assailant's face. Quarter beat strikes are primarily responsible for creating the psychological panic and trauma when Razing.

R

range—The spatial relationship between a fighter and a threatening assailant.

range deficiency—The inability to effectively fight and defend in all ranges of combat (armed and unarmed).

range manipulation—A combative attribute. The strategic manipulation of combat ranges.

range proficiency—A combative attribute. The ability to effectively fight and defend in all ranges of combat (armed and unarmed).

ranges of engagement—See combat ranges.

ranges of unarmed combat—The three distances (kicking range, punching range, and grappling range) a fighter might physically engage with an assailant while involved in unarmed combat.

raze – To level, demolish or obliterate.

razer – One who performs the Razing methodology.

razing – The second phase of the Widow Maker Program. A series of vicious close quarter techniques designed to physically and psychologically extirpate a criminal attacker.

razing amplifier - a technique, tactic or procedure that magnifies the destructiveness of your razing technique.

reaction dynamics—see probable reaction dynamics.

reaction time—The elapsed time between a stimulus and the response to that particular stimulus. See offensive reaction time and defensive reaction time.

rear cross—A straight punch delivered from the rear hand that crosses from right to left (if in a left stance) or left to right (if in a right stance).

rear side—The side of the body furthest from the assailant. See lead side.

reasonable force—That degree of force which is not excessive for a particular event and which is appropriate in protecting yourself or others.

refinement—The strategic and methodical process of improving or perfecting.

relocation principle—Also known as relocating, this is a street-fighting tactic that requires you to immediately move to a new location (usually by flanking your adversary) after delivering a compound attack.

repetition—Performing a single movement, exercise, strike, or action continuously for a specific period.

research—A scientific investigation or inquiry.

rhythm—Movements characterized by the natural ebb and flow of related elements.

ritual-oriented training—Formalized training that is conducted without intrinsic purpose. See combat-oriented training and sport-oriented training.

S

safety—One of the three criteria for a CFA body weapon, technique, maneuver, or tactic. It means that the tool, technique, maneuver or tactic provides the least amount of danger and risk for the practitioner. See efficiency and effectiveness.

scissors hold—See guard position.

scorching – Quickly and inconspicuously applying oleoresin capsicum (hot pepper extract) on your fingertips and then razing your adversary.

self-awareness—One of the three categories of CFA awareness. Knowing and understanding yourself. This includes aspects of yourself which may provoke criminal violence and which will promote a proper and strong reaction to an attack. See criminal awareness and situational awareness.

self-confidence—Having trust and faith in yourself.

self-enlightenment—The state of knowing your capabilities, limitations, character traits, feelings, general attributes, and motivations. See self-awareness.

set—A term used to describe a grouping of repetitions.

shadow fighting—A CFA training exercise used to develop and refine your tools, techniques, and attributes of armed and unarmed combat.

sharking – A counter attack technique that is used when your adversary grabs your razing hand.

shielding wedge - a defensive maneuver used to counter an unarmed postal attack.

simple direct attack (SDA) – One of the five methods of attack. A method of attack whereby the practitioner delivers a solitary offenses tool or technique. It may involve a series of discrete probes or one swift, powerful strike aimed at terminating the encounter.

situational awareness—One of the three categories of CFA awareness. A state of being totally alert to your immediate surroundings, including people, places, objects, and actions. (See criminal awareness and self-awareness.)

skeletal alignment—The proper alignment or arrangement of your body. Skeletal alignment maximizes the structural integrity of striking tools.

skills—One of the three factors that determine who will win a street fight. Skills refers to psychomotor proficiency with the tools and techniques of combat. See Attitude and Knowledge.

slipping—A defensive maneuver that permits you to avoid an assailant's linear blow without stepping out of range. Slipping can be accomplished by quickly snapping the head and upper torso sideways (right or left) to avoid the blow.

snap back—A defensive maneuver that permits you to avoid an assailant's linear and circular blows without stepping out of range. The snap back can be accomplished by quickly snapping the head backward to avoid the assailant's blow.

somatotypes—A method of classifying human body types or builds into three different categories: endomorph, mesomorph, and ectomorph. See endomorph, mesomorph, and ectomorph.

sparring—A training exercise where two or more fighters fight each other while wearing protective equipment.

speed—A physical attribute of armed and unarmed combat. The rate or a measure of the rapid rate of motion.

spiritual component—One of the three vital components of the CFA system. The spiritual component includes the metaphysical issues and aspects of existence. See physical component and mental component.

sport-oriented training—Training that is geared for competition and governed by a set of rules. See combat-oriented training and ritual-oriented training.

sprawling—A grappling technique used to counter a double- or single-leg takedown.

square off—To be face-to-face with a hostile or threatening assailant who is about to attack you.

stance—One of the many strategic postures you assume prior to or during armed or unarmed combat.

stick fighting—Fighting that takes place with either one or two sticks.

strategic positioning—Tactically positioning yourself to either escape, move behind a barrier, or use a makeshift weapon.

strategic/tactical development—One of the five elements of CFA's mental component.

strategy—A carefully planned method of achieving your goal of engaging an assailant under advantageous conditions.

street fight—A spontaneous and violent confrontation between two or more individuals wherein no rules apply.

street fighter—An unorthodox combatant who has no formal training. His combative skills and tactics are usually developed in the street by the process of trial and error.

street training—A CFA training methodology requiring the practitioner to deliver explosive compound attacks for 10 to 20 seconds. See condition ng training and proficiency training.

strength training—The process of developing muscular strength through systematic application of progressive resistance.

striking art—A combat art that relies predominantly on striking techniques to neutralize or terminate a criminal attacker.

striking shield—A rectangular shield constructed of foam and vinyl used to develop power in your kicks, punches, and strikes.

striking tool—A natural body weapon that impacts with the assailant's anatomical target.

strong side—The strongest and most coordinated side of your body.

structure—A definite and organized pattern.

style—The distinct manner in which a fighter executes or performs his combat skills.

stylistic integration—The purposeful and scientific collection of tools and techniques from various disciplines, which are strategically integrated and dramatically altered to meet three essential criteria: efficiency, effectiveness, and combative safety.

submission holds—Also known as control and restraint techniques, many of these locks and holds create sufficient pain to cause the adversary to submit.

system—The unification of principles, philosophies, rules, strategies, methodologies, tools, and techniques of a particular method of combat.

T

tactic—The skill of using the available means to achieve an end.

target awareness—A combative attribute that encompasses five strategic principles: target orientation, target recognition, target selection, target impaction, and target exploitation.

target exploitation—A combative attribute. The strategic maximization of your assailant's reaction dynamics during a fight. Target exploitation can be applied in both armed and unarmed encounters.

target impaction—The successful striking of the appropriate anatomical target.

target orientation—A combative attribute. Having a workable knowledge of the assailant's anatomical targets.

target recognition—The ability to immediately recognize appropriate anatomical targets during an emergency self-defense situation.

target selection—The process of mentally selecting the appropriate anatomical target for your self-defense situation. This is predicated on certain factors, including proper force response, assailant's positioning, and range.

target stare—A form of telegraphing in which you stare at the anatomical target you intend to strike.

target zones—The three areas in which an assailant's anatomical targets are located. (See zone one, zone two and zone three.)

technique—A systematic procedure by which a task is accomplished.

telegraphic cognizance—A combative attribute. The ability to recognize both verbal and non-verbal signs of aggression or assault.

telegraphing—Unintentionally making your intentions known to your adversary.

tempo—The speed or rate at which you speak.

terminate—To kill.

terror—The third stage of fear; defined as overpowering fear. See fright and panic.

timing—A physical and mental attribute of armed and unarmed combat. Your ability to execute a movement at the optimum moment.

tone—The overall quality or character of your voice.

tool—See body weapon.

traditional martial arts—Any martial art that fails to evolve and change to meet the demands and characteristics of its present environment.

traditional style/system—See traditional martial arts.

training drills—The various exercises and drills aimed at perfecting combat skills, attributes, and tactics.

trap and tuck – A counter move technique used when the adversary attempts to raze you during your quarter beat assault.

U

unified mind—A mind free and clear of distractions and focused on the combative situation.

use of force response—A combative attribute. Selecting the appropriate level of force for a particular emergency self-defense situation.

V

viciousness—A combative attribute. The propensity to be extremely violent and destructive often characterized by intense savagery.

violence—The intentional utilization of physical force to coerce, injure, cripple, or kill.

visualization—Also known as mental visualization or mental imagery. The purposeful formation of mental images and scenarios in the mind's eye.

W

warm-up—A series of mild exercises, stretches, and movements designed to prepare you for more intense exercise.

weak side—The weaker and more uncoordinated side of your body.

weapon and technique mastery—A component of CFA's physical component. The kinesthetic and psychomotor development of a weapon or combative technique.

weapon capability—An assailant's ability to use and attack with a particular weapon.

webbing - The first phase of the Widow Maker Program. Webbing is a two hand strike delivered to the assailant's chin. It is called Webbing because your hands resemble a large web that wraps around the enemy's face.

widow maker – One who makes widows by destroying husbands.

widow maker program – A CFA combat program specifically designed to teach the law abiding citizen how to use extreme force when faced with immediate threat of unlawful deadly criminal attack. The Widow Maker program is divided into two phases or methodologies: Webbing and Razing.

Y

yell—A loud and aggressive scream or shout used for various strategic reasons.

Z

zero beat – One of the four beat classifications of the Widow Maker, Feral Fighting and Savage Street Fighting Programs. Zero beat strikes are full pressure techniques applied to a specific target until it completely ruptures. They include gouging, crushing, biting, and choking techniques.

zone one—Anatomical targets related to your senses, including the eyes, temple, nose, chin, and back of neck.

zone three—Anatomical targets related to your mobility, including thighs, knees, shins, and instep.

zone two—Anatomical targets related to your breathing, including front of neck, solar plexus, ribs, and groin.

The 10 Best Bar Fighting Moves

About Sammy Franco

With over 30 years of experience, Sammy Franco is one of the world's foremost authorities on armed and unarmed self-defense. Highly regarded as a leading innovator in combat sciences, Mr. Franco was one of the premier pioneers in the field of "reality-based" self-defense and martial arts instruction.

Sammy Franco is perhaps best known as the founder and creator of Contemporary Fighting Arts (CFA), a state-of-the-art offensive-based combat system that is specifically designed for real-world self-defense. CFA is a sophisticated and practical system of self-defense, designed specifically to provide efficient and effective methods to avoid, defuse, confront, and neutralize both armed and unarmed attackers.

Sammy Franco has frequently been featured in martial art magazines, newspapers, and appeared on numerous radio and television programs. Mr. Franco has also authored numerous books, magazine articles, and editorials, and has developed a popular library of instructional videos.

Sammy Franco's experience and credibility in the combat sciences is unequaled. One of his many accomplishments in this field includes the fact that he has earned the ranking of a Law Enforcement Master Instructor, and has designed, implemented, and taught officer survival training to the United States Border Patrol (USBP). He has instructed members of the US Secret Service, Military Special Forces,

Washington DC Police Department, Montgomery County, Maryland Deputy Sheriffs, and the US Library of Congress Police. Sammy Franco is also a member of the prestigious International Law Enforcement Educators and Trainers Association (ILEETA) as well as the American Society of Law Enforcement Trainers (ASLET) and he is listed in the "Who's Who Director of Law Enforcement Instructors."

Sammy Franco is a nationally certified Law Enforcement Instructor in the following curricula: PR-24 Side-Handle Baton, Police Arrest and Control Procedures, Police Personal Weapons Tactics, Police Power Handcuffing Methods, Police Oleoresin Capsicum Aerosol Training (OCAT), Police Weapon Retention and Disarming Methods, Police Edged Weapon Countermeasures and "Use of Force" Assessment and Response Methods.

Mr. Franco holds a Bachelor of Arts degree in Criminal Justice from the University of Maryland. He is a regularly featured speaker at a number of professional conferences and conducts dynamic and enlightening seminars on numerous aspects of self-defense and combat training.

On a personal level, Sammy Franco is an animal lover, who will go to great lengths to assist and rescue animals. Throughout the years, he's rescued everything from turkey vultures to goats. However, his most treasured moments are always spent with his beloved German Shepherd dogs.

For more information about Mr. Franco and his unique Contemporary Fighting Arts system, you can visit his website at: **SammyFranco.com** or follow him on twitter **@RealSammyFranco**

Other Books by Sammy Franco

THE WIDOW MAKER PROGRAM
Extreme Self-Defense for Deadly Force Situations
by Sammy Franco

The Widow Maker Program is a shocking and revolutionary fighting style designed to unleash extreme force when faced with the immediate threat of an unlawful deadly criminal attack. In this unique book, self-defense innovator Sammy Franco teaches you his brutal and unorthodox combat style that is virtually indefensible and utterly devastating. With over 250 photographs and detailed step-by-step instructions, The Widow Maker Program teaches you Franco's surreptitious Webbing and Razing techniques. When combined, these two fighting methods create an unstoppable force capable of destroying the toughest adversary. 8.5 x 5.5, paperback, photos, illus, 218 pages.

INVINCIBLE
Mental Toughness Techniques for
Peak Performance
by Sammy Franco

Invincible is a treasure trove of battle-tested techniques and strategies for improving mental toughness in all aspects of life. It teaches you how to unlock the true power of your mind and achieve success in sports, fitness, high-risk professions, self-defense, and other peak performance activities. However, you don't have to be an athlete or warrior to benefit from this unique mental toughness book. In fact, the mental skills featured in this indispensable program can be used by anyone who wants to reach their full potential in life. 8.5 x 5.5, paperback, photos, illus, 250 pages.

MAXIMUM DAMAGE
Hidden Secrets Behind Brutal
Fighting Combination
by Sammy Franco

Maximum Damage teaches you the quickest ways to beat your opponent in the street by exploiting his physical and psychological reactions in a fight. Learn how to stay two steps ahead of your adversary by knowing exactly how he will react to your strikes before they are delivered. In this unique book, reality based self-defense expert Sammy Franco reveals his unique Probable Reaction Dynamic (PRD) fighting method. Probable reaction dynamics are both a scientific and comprehensive offensive strategy based on the positional theory of combat. Regardless of your style of fighting, PRD training will help you overpower your opponent by seamlessly integrating your strikes into brutal fighting combinations that are fast, ferocious and final! 8.5 x 5.5, paperback, 240 photos, illustrations, 238 pages.

SAVAGE STREET FIGHTING
Tactical Savagery as a Last Resort
by Sammy Franco

In this revolutionary book, Sammy Franco reveals the science behind his most primal street fighting method. Savage Street Fighting is a brutal self-defense system specifically designed to teach the law-abiding citizen how to use "Tactical Savagery" when faced with the immediate threat of an unlawful deadly criminal attack. Savage Street Fighting is systematically engineered to protect you when there are no other self-defense options left! With over 300 photographs and detailed step-by-step instructions, Savage Street Fighting is a must-have book for anyone concerned about real world self-defense. Now is the time to learn how to unleash your inner beast! 8.5 x 5.5, paperback, 317 photos, illustrations, 232 pages.

FIRST STRIKE
End a Fight in Ten Seconds or Less!
by Sammy Franco

Learn how to stop any attack before it starts by mastering the art of the preemptive strike. First Strike gives you an easy-to-learn yet highly effective self-defense game plan for handling violent close-quarter combat encounters. First Strike will teach you instinctive, practical and realistic self-defense techniques that will drop any criminal attacker to the floor with one punishing blow. By reading this book and by practicing, you will learn the hard-hitting skills necessary to execute a punishing first strike and ultimately prevail in a self-defense situation. And that's what it is all about: winning in as little time as possible. 8.5 x 5.5, paperback, photos, illustrations, 202 pages.

WAR MACHINE
How to Transform Yourself Into A Vicious & Deadly Street Fighter
by Sammy Franco

War Machine is a book that will change you for the rest of your life! When followed accordingly, War Machine will forge your mind, body and spirit into iron. Once armed with the mental and physical attributes of the War Machine, you will become a strong and confident warrior that can handle just about anything that life may throw your way. In essence, War

Machine is a way of life. Powerful, intense, and hard. 11 x 8.5, paperback, photos, illustrations, 210 pages.

KUBOTAN POWER
Quick and Simple Steps to Mastering the Kubotan Keychain
by Sammy Franco

With over 290 photographs and step-by-step instructions, Kubotan Power is the authoritative resource for mastering this devastating self-defense weapon. In this one-of-a-kind book, world-renowned self-defense expert, Sammy Franco takes thirty years of real-world teaching experience and gives you quick, easy and practical kubotan techniques that can be used by civilians, law enforcement personnel, or military professionals. The Kubotan is an incredible self-defense weapon that has helped thousands of people effectively defend themselves. Men, women, law enforcement officers, military, and security professionals alike, appreciate this small and discreet self-defense tool. Unfortunately, however, very little has been written about the kubotan, leaving it shrouded in both mystery and ignorance. As a result, most people don't know how to unleash the full power of this unique personal defense weapon. 8.5 x 5.5, paperback, 290 photos, illustrations, 204 pages.

THE COMPLETE BODY OPPONENT BAG BOOK
by Sammy Franco

In this one-of-a-kind book, Sammy Franco teaches you the many hidden training features of the body opponent bag that will improve your fighting skills and boost your conditioning. With detailed photographs, step-by-step instructions, and dozens of unique workout routines, The Complete Body Opponent Bag Book is the authoritative resource for mastering this lifelike punching bag. The Complete Body Opponent Bag Book covers stances, punching, kicking, grappling techniques, mobility and footwork, targets, fighting ranges, training gear, time based workouts, punching and kicking combinations, weapons training, grappling drills, ground fighting, and dozens of workouts that will challenge you for years to come. 8.5 x 5.5, paperback, 139 photos, illustrations, 206 pages.

CONTEMPORARY FIGHTING ARTS, LLC
"Real World Self-Defense Since 1989"
www.SammyFranco.com

CPSIA information can be obtained
at www.ICGtesting.com
Printed in the USA
LVOW03s1030080418
572687LV00005B/871/P